¡Así se dice!

Glencoe Spanish 1

Pre-AP* Workbook

Reina Martínez

The *McGraw·Hill* Companies

 **Glencoe**

Send all inquiries to:
Glencoe/McGraw-Hill
8787 Orion Place
Columbus, OH 43240-4027

ISBN: 978-0-07-888940-0
MHID: 0-07-888940-5

Printed in the United States of America.

9 10 QLM 14

Contenido

Capítulo 1 1

Capítulo 2 17

Capítulo 3 33

Capítulo 4 49

Capítulo 5 65

Capítulo 6 81

Capítulo 7 97

Capítulo 8 113

Capítulo 9 129

Capítulo 10 145

Capítulo 11 161

¿Cómo somos?

CAPÍTULO ❶ ¿Cómo somos?

Short Dialogue 

Directions: You will now listen to an audio selection. You may take notes in the space provided. At the end of the selection, you will be asked some questions about what you have just heard. Select the best answer to each question from among the four choices printed in your booklet.

This dialogue is an imaginary conversation between the characters Don Quijote and Sancho Panza.

Voices in the dialogue:

Narrator, Don Quijote, Sancho Panza

Write your notes here.

____

____

____

____

____

____

____

❶ a. tonto
  b. inteligente
  c. perezoso
  d. absurdo

❷ a. inteligente
  b. ambicioso
  c. perezoso
  d. absurdo

❸ a. They are synonyms.
  b. They are NOT words used to describe people.
  c. They are antonyms.
  d. They are both used to describe Sancho.

❹ a. Don Quijote and Sancho do not agree.
  b. Don Quijote and Sancho do agree.
  c. Sancho is as hard-working as Don Quijote.
  d. Don Quijote is not hard-working.

Short Narrative 🎧

Directions: You will now listen to an audio selection. You may take notes in the space provided. At the end of the selection, you will be asked some questions about what you have just heard. Select the best answer to each question from among the four choices printed in your booklet.

This narrative is about a Spanish-speaking student.

Voices in the narrative:

Narrator

Write your notes here.

____

____

____

____

____

____

1
a. mexicana
b. colombiana
c. tropical
d. puertorriqueña

2
a. un colegio
b. una alumna
c. la capital de Puerto Rico
d. una península

3
a. una persona graciosa
b. una alumna mala
c. ambiciosa
d. una alumna seria

4
a. tropical
b. una península
c. un colegio
d. la capital

CAPÍTULO ❶ ¿Cómo somos?

Reading Comprehension

Directions: Read the following passage carefully for comprehension. The passage is followed by a number of incomplete statements or questions. Select the completion or answer that is best according to the passage.

This is a reading about Simón Bolívar.

Simón Bolívar es un héroe famoso de Latinoamérica. Es de una familia noble y rica de Venezuela. No es de la ciudad. Simón Bolívar es de una región rural. Es del campo.

En la época de Simón Bolívar, Venezuela es una colonia de España. No es una nación independiente. La mayoría de Latinoamérica es una colonia española. Las ideas de Simón Bolívar son muy liberales. Para él, Venezuela no debe[1] ser una colonia. Venezuela debe ser una nación independiente.

[1]debe   *should*

 **1** What is the main idea of this reading?

   a. Simón Bolívar is from a rich family.

   b. Most of Latin America used to be a Spanish colony.

   c. Simón Bolívar is considered a hero of Latin America.

   d. Venezuela was not a Spanish colony.

2 Based on the reading, which of the following is true?

   a. Simón Bolívar wanted to see Venezuela become a free country.

   b. Simón Bolívar didn't like rural life.

   c. Simón Bolívar wanted Venezuela to remain a Spanish colony.

   d. Simón Bolívar didn't like being from a rich and noble family.

3 Based on the reading, we know that Bolívar is from…

   a. Spain.

   b. a rural part of Venezuela.

   c. a big city.

   d. a liberal family.

4 What conclusion can you draw based on the following sentences?

Las ideas de Simón Bolívar son muy liberales. Para él, Venezuela no debe ser una colonia. Venezuela debe ser una nación independiente.

   a. Bolívar never expressed his liberal ideas.

   b. Not everyone believed that Venezuela should become an independent country.

   c. Bolívar wanted to leave Venezuela.

   d. Bolívar didn't believe that Venezuela could become an independent country.

Paragraph Completion (with root words)

Directions: Read the following passage. Then write, on the line after each number, the form of the word in parentheses needed to complete the passage correctly, logically, and grammatically. Be sure to spell and accent the word correctly. You may have to use more than one word in some cases, but you must use a form of the word given in parentheses. Be sure to write the word on the line even if no change is needed.

¡Hola! Nosotros __1__ de la República Dominicana. Mi amigo Pedro __2__ de San Francisco de Macorís y yo __3__ de Puerto Plata, __4__ ciudad en __5__ costa norte de la República Dominicana. Somos __6__ amigos. Mi amigo Pedro, __7__ joven inteligente y serio, __8__ un alumno bueno. Somos alumnos en la misma escuela. __9__ escuela es el colegio Juan Pablo Duarte en Santiago. Es una preparatoria muy __10__.

1. _______________________ (ser)
2. _______________________ (ser)
3. _______________________ (ser)
4. _______________________ (un)
5. _______________________ (el)
6. _______________________ (bueno)
7. _______________________ (un)
8. _______________________ (ser)
9. _______________________ (el)
10. _______________________ (famoso)

Colombia __1__ una nación hispanohablante en el norte de __2__ América del Sur. Juanes __3__ de Medellín, una ciudad __4__. Juanes __5__ un cantante[1] popular de música __6__. El nombre completo de Juanes __7__ Juan Esteban. __8__ canción[2] famosa de Juanes __9__ «A Dios le Pido». Juanes es muy __10__.

1. _______________________ (ser)
2. _______________________ (el)
3. _______________________ (ser)
4. _______________________ (colombiano)
5. _______________________ (ser)
6. _______________________ (hispano)
7. _______________________ (ser)
8. _______________________ (Un)
9. _______________________ (ser)
10. _______________________ (simpático)

[1]cantante *singer*   [2]canción *song*

Paragraph Completion (without root words)

Directions: First read the passage and then write, on the line after each number, an appropriate word to complete the passage correctly, logically, and grammatically. Be sure to spell and accent the word correctly. Only ONE Spanish word should be inserted. You will have to use nouns, articles, adjectives, verbs, etc.

Carlos y Teresa _____1_____ alumnos en _____2_____ escuela secundaria en Lima, la capital de Perú. Perú _____3_____ una nación en la América del Sur. Ellos son _____4_____ muy buenos. _____5_____ clase de español _____6_____ muy interesante y _____7_____ profesora de español es simpática. Carlos y Teresa _____8_____ alumnos y amigos.

1. _______________________
2. _______________________
3. _______________________
4. _______________________
5. _______________________
6. _______________________
7. _______________________
8. _______________________

Informal Writing

Directions: For the following question, you will write a message. Your response should be at least 20 words in length.

You are writing an e-mail to Carlos. You met him while vacationing in Mexico. He wants to know what your best friend is like. Describe your friend in detail. You may want to

- tell who your friend is
- tell where he/she is from
- describe your friend's physical traits
- describe your friend's personality

Formal Writing

Directions: The following question is based on the Sources (**Fuentes**) 1–3. The first two sources are readings. Fill in the graphic organizer when you have finished reading them. You will hear audio material for the third source. Take notes as you listen. Then you will plan your response to the question. Your response should be at least 25 words in length.

Compare and contrast Alicia, Jorge, and Felipe. How are they similar? How are they different?

Formal Writing

Fuente 1 Una alumna venezolana

Alicia Bustelo es una muchacha venezolana. Ella es de Caracas, la capital de Venezuela. Alicia es alta y morena. Es muy graciosa. Pero es también una alumna seria. Es alumna en el Colegio Simón Bolívar. En Latinoamérica un colegio es una escuela secundaria. El Colegio Simón Bolívar es una escuela muy buena.

Formal Writing

Fuente 2 Un e-mail

¡Hola!

Soy Jorge Pérez Navarro. Soy de Madrid, la capital de España. Soy español. Soy alumno en el Colegio Sorolla. Soy rubio y bastante alto. Soy bastante gracioso. No soy muy serio. No soy tímido. De ninguna manera.

Hasta pronto,

Jorge

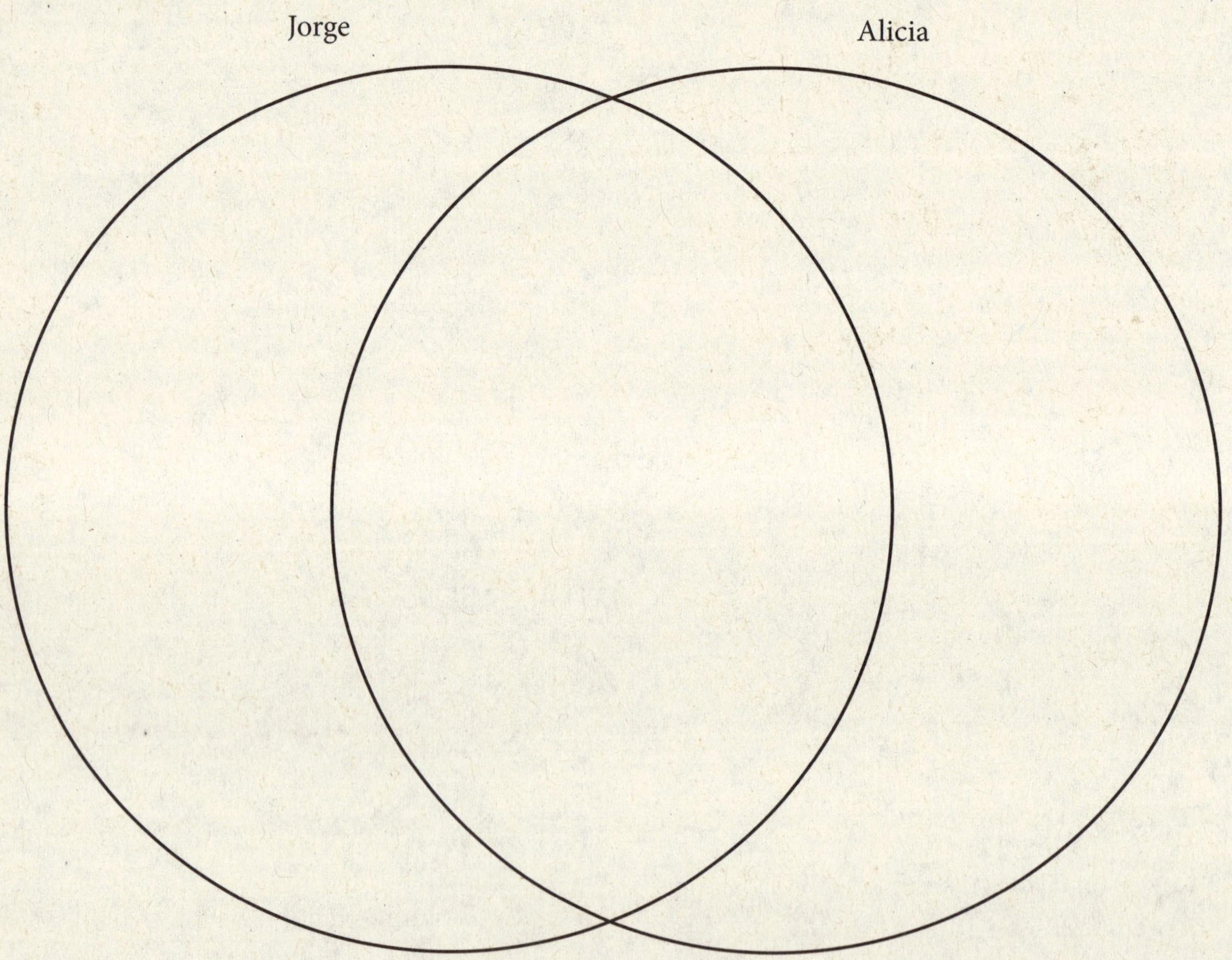

Formal Writing

Fuente 3 🎧 The following dialogue between friends takes place at school.

Voices in the dialogue:

Rafael, José, Felipe

Write your notes here.

Informal Speaking 🎧

Directions: You will participate in a simulated conversation. First, read the outline of the conversation. You will have 20 seconds to respond to each question. Once the conversation begins, a tone will indicate when you should begin and end speaking. You should participate in the conversation as fully and appropriately as possible.

You are answering a newspaper ad about a summer job. You call the company. You are being interviewed by telephone for the job by Mr. Sánchez who will ask you several questions.

La conversación The shaded lines reflect what you will be hearing on the recording.

Sr. Sánchez:	Greets you and asks your name.
Tú:	Greet him and tell him your name.
Sr. Sánchez:	He asks you a question.
Tú:	Answer him.
Sr. Sánchez:	He asks you a question.
Tú:	Answer him.
Sr. Sánchez:	He asks you a final question.
Tú:	Answer him.
Sr. Sánchez:	Says good-bye.
Tú:	Say good-bye.

CAPÍTULO 1 ¿Cómo somos? ···○

Formal Oral Presentation

Directions: The following question is based on the accompanying printed article and audio selection. First, you will read the article. Then, you will hear the audio selection. You should take notes while you listen. You will then respond to the statement below ORALLY.

Compare and contrast the groups of students from the reading and audio selection. Then, talk about what you have in common with them. You may want to use the graphic organizer below to organize your thoughts.

Roberto y Alberto	Francisco y Guadalupe	Ramón y Marisa

Formal Oral Presentation

Fuente 1 Hermanos latinos de Nueva York

¡Saludos desde la Ciudad de Nueva York! Somos Roberto y Alberto Martínez. Somos hermanos y somos de ascendencia dominicana pero somos de Nueva York. El español es una lengua muy importante en Nueva York porque hay muchos dominicanos; pero no hay solo hispanohablantes dominicanos. En Nueva York, hay hispanohablantes de todas las naciones de Latinoamérica y del Caribe.

Fuente 2 🎧 This article is titled **Amigos latinos en Estados Unidos.**

Voices in the narrative:

Narrator

Write your notes here.

____

____

____

____

____

____

____

____

____

____

____

____

____

____

La familia y la casa

Short Dialogue 🎧

Directions: You will now listen to an audio selection. You may take notes in the space provided. At the end of the selection, you will be asked some questions about what you have just heard. Select the best answer to each question from among the four choices printed in your booklet.

The following is a conversation between two classmates.

Voices in the dialogue:

Narrator, Teresa, Ernesto

Write your notes here.

____

____

____

____

____

____

____

1
a. He has a brother and a dog.
b. He is older than his sister.
c. He has a sister and a dog.
d. He is the youngest child in his family.

2
a. She is fourteen years old.
b. She has a dog.
c. She has a sister.
d. We do not learn any information about Teresa.

3
a. Tiene catorce años.
b. Tiene dieciséis años.
c. Tiene una gata.
d. No tiene una gata.

4
a. No, no tiene una mascota.
b. Sí, tiene un perrito.
c. Sí, tiene una gata.
d. Sí, tiene un perrito y una gata.

CAPÍTULO ❷ La familia y la casa ·······························o

Short Narrative 🎧

Directions: You will now listen to an audio selection. You may take notes in the space provided. At the end of the selection, you will be asked some questions about what you have just heard. Select the best answer to each question from among the four choices printed in your booklet.

You will hear an advertisement on a local Spanish radio station.

Voices in the narrative:

Narrator, Announcer

Write your notes here.

____

____

____

____

____

❶ **a.** a house
   b. an apartment
   c. an apartment building
   d. an agency

❷ **a.** in the suburbs
   b. on Main Street
   c. in the city center
   d. in the countryside

❸ **a.** Benavides
   b. Bolívar
   c. Bogotá
   d. Avenida

❹ **a.** 2
   b. 3
   c. 7
   d. 20

❺ **a.** It has a modern kitchen.
   b. It has several balconies.
   c. It has a private elevator.
   d. It has a great price.

CAPÍTULO 2 La familia y la casa

Reading Comprehension

Directions: Read the following passage carefully for comprehension. The passage is followed by a number of incomplete statements or questions. Select the completion or answer that is best according to the passage.

This reading is about indigenous civilizations in Latin America.

En muchas partes de Latinoamérica hay influencias importantes de las poblaciones indígenas. Antes de la llegada[1] de Cristóbal Colón a las Américas, los habitantes de la América del Norte, de la América Central y de la América del Sur son los indígenas.

Hoy hay descendientes de los famosos aztecas y mayas en México, Guatemala y otras partes de la América Central.

En países como Ecuador, Perú y Bolivia hay muchos descendientes de los incas. Y más al sur en Chile hay descendientes de los araucanos. Pero hay muy pocos.

[1]llegada *arrival*

1 When did indigenous civilizations inhabit Latin America?

a. after the arrival of Christopher Columbus

b. before the arrival of Christopher Columbus

c. Indigenous populations never inhabited Latin America.

d. The article doesn't mention when they inhabited Latin America.

2 In the article, **las Américas** refers to...

a. North America

b. Canada and Mexico

c. North America, Central America, and South America

d. Latin America

3 Based on the article, we know that the Aztecs and Mayans lived where?

a. in Mexico and parts of Central America

b. in Peru, Ecuador, and Bolivia

c. in Chile

d. in all parts of Latin America

4 What conclusion can be made based on the following sentences?

Y más al sur en Chile hay descendientes de los araucanos. Pero hay muy pocos.

a. The Araucano population was never very large.

b. There are not a lot of descendents of the Araucanos left.

c. No one knows what happened to the Araucanos.

d. Chile does not have a large population.

CAPÍTULO ② La familia y la casa

5 Why is **Cristóbal Colón** mentioned in the article?

   a. He was a famous Native American.

   b. He was a European credited with the discovery of America.

   c. He was a popular activist.

   d. He was a Spanish author.

CAPÍTULO 2 La familia y la casa

Paragraph Completion (with root words)

Directions: Read the following passage. Then write, on the line after each number, the form of the word in parentheses needed to complete the passage correctly, logically, and grammatically. Be sure to spell and accent the word correctly. You may have to use more than one word in some cases, but you must use a form of the word given in parentheses. Be sure to write the word on the line even if no change is needed.

—Daniel, ¿____1____ hermanos?

—Sí, (nosotros) ____2____ tres. Yo ____3____ un hermano y ____4____ hermana. Ellos son ____5____ hermanos muy ____6____. Mi hermano ____7____ muy interesante. Él es ____8____ de español. ____9____ hermana es ____10____. Ella tiene solo quince años.

1. _______________________ (tener)
2. _______________________ (ser)
3. _______________________ (tener)
4. _______________________ (un)
5. _______________________ (un)
6. _______________________ (bueno)
7. _______________________ (ser)
8. _______________________ (profesor)
9. _______________________ (mi)
10. _______________________ (simpático)

Aquí nosotros ____1____ una foto de la familia Ramos. Hay cuatro personas en ____2____ familia Ramos. También, (ellos) ____3____ una perrita ____4____. La familia ____5____ un apartamento muy ____6____ en Salamanca—____7____ zona bastante ____8____ de Madrid. ____9____ apartamento tiene seis cuartos. La familia Ramos también tiene ____10____ casa de campo en Chinchón.

1. _______________________ (tener)
2. _______________________ (el)
3. _______________________ (tener)
4. _______________________ (cariñoso)
5. _______________________ (tener)
6. _______________________ (bonito)
7. _______________________ (un)
8. _______________________ (elegante)
9. _______________________ (el)
10. _______________________ (un)

CAPÍTULO ② La familia y la casa ·································○

Paragraph Completion (without root words)

Directions: First read the passage and then write, on the line after each number, an appropriate word to complete the passage correctly, logically, and grammatically. Be sure to spell and accent the word correctly. Only ONE Spanish word should be inserted. You will have to use nouns, articles, adjectives, verbs, etc.

En mi familia hay cinco personas. Mi padre, ___1___ madre, mis dos hermanos y ___2___. Tengo dieciséis ___3___. Nosotros ___4___ una casa muy bonita en Sevilla. La casa ___5___ cuatro habitaciones, ___6___ cocina, una sala grande y dos baños.

1. _________________________

2. _________________________

3. _________________________

4. _________________________

5. _________________________

6. _________________________

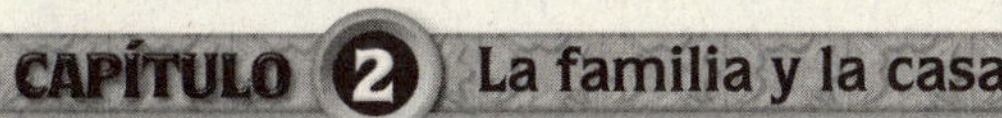

CAPÍTULO ② La familia y la casa

Informal Writing

Directions: For the following question, you will write a message. Your response should be at least 25 words in length.

You are writing an e-mail to your key pal from Venezuela. He wants to know about your family and your home. You may want to

- tell how many people are in your family
- describe the members of your family
- tell how old they are
- describe your house

Formal Writing

Directions: The following question is based on the Sources (**Fuentes**) 1–3. The first two sources are readings. Fill in the graphic organizer when you have finished reading them. You will hear audio material for the third source. Take notes as you listen. Then you will plan your response to the question. Your response should be at least 25 words in length.

Who appears in the family picture described in each of the sources? Tell who is in your family picture and describe each person.

CAPÍTULO ② La familia y la casa ·······································o

Formal Writing

Fuente 1 Una foto de la familia Valero

Aquí tengo una foto de la familia de Elena Valero. En la foto hay ocho personas: los padres, los hijos y los abuelos. Es una familia grande. Los padres de Elena son Pedro y Susana. Elena tiene tres hermanos mayores—Ricardo, Víctor y Alex. Ella es la menor. Los abuelos de Elena son muy simpáticos. Ellos son Raúl y Ana. La familia es de Panamá.

Formal Writing

Fuente 2 Una foto de la familia Montero

En la foto hay cinco personas. Es una familia que no es muy grande, pero no es una familia pequeña. Es la familia de Jorge y Niza Montero. Ellos son profesores en una escuela en la Florida. Sus hijos—Sandra, Samuel y Emilia— son muy inteligentes y simpáticos. Los Montero son de la Florida. Son de nacionalidad cubana. Su hija mayor, Sandra, tiene diez años. Su hijo, Samuel, tiene ocho años. Y la menor, Emilia, tiene cuatro años.

La foto de la familia Valero	La foto de la familia Montero

CAPÍTULO 2 La familia y la casa

Formal Writing

Fuente 3 🎧 The narrative gives information about a famous painting or "photo" of a royal family.

Voices in the narrative:

Narrator

Write your notes here.

____

____

____

____

____

____

____

____

____

____

____

____

____

____

____

____

____

Informal Speaking 🎧

Directions: You will participate in a simulated conversation. First, read the outline of the conversation. You will have 20 seconds to respond to each question. Once the conversation begins, a tone will indicate when you should begin and end speaking. You should participate in the conversation as fully and appropriately as possible.

Imagine you are being interviewed by the popular talk show host Cristina on her show. She wants to know more about you.

La conversación The shaded lines reflect what you will be hearing on the recording.

Cristina:	Greets you and asks you a question.
Tú:	Greet her and answer.
Cristina:	Asks you a question about your family.
Tú:	Answer her.
Cristina:	Asks you a question about your parents.
Tú:	Answer her.
Cristina:	Asks you a question about your siblings.
Tú:	Answer her.
Cristina:	Asks you a question about your house.
Tú:	Answer her.
Cristina:	Asks you a final question.
Tú:	Answer her.
Cristina:	Thanks you.
Tú:	Thank her.

Formal Oral Presentation

Directions: The following question is based on the accompanying printed article and audio selection. First, you will read the article. Then, you will hear the audio selection. You should take notes while you listen. You will then respond to the statement below ORALLY.

Describe the families and their houses. How do they compare with your family? You may want to use the graphic organizer to organize your thoughts.

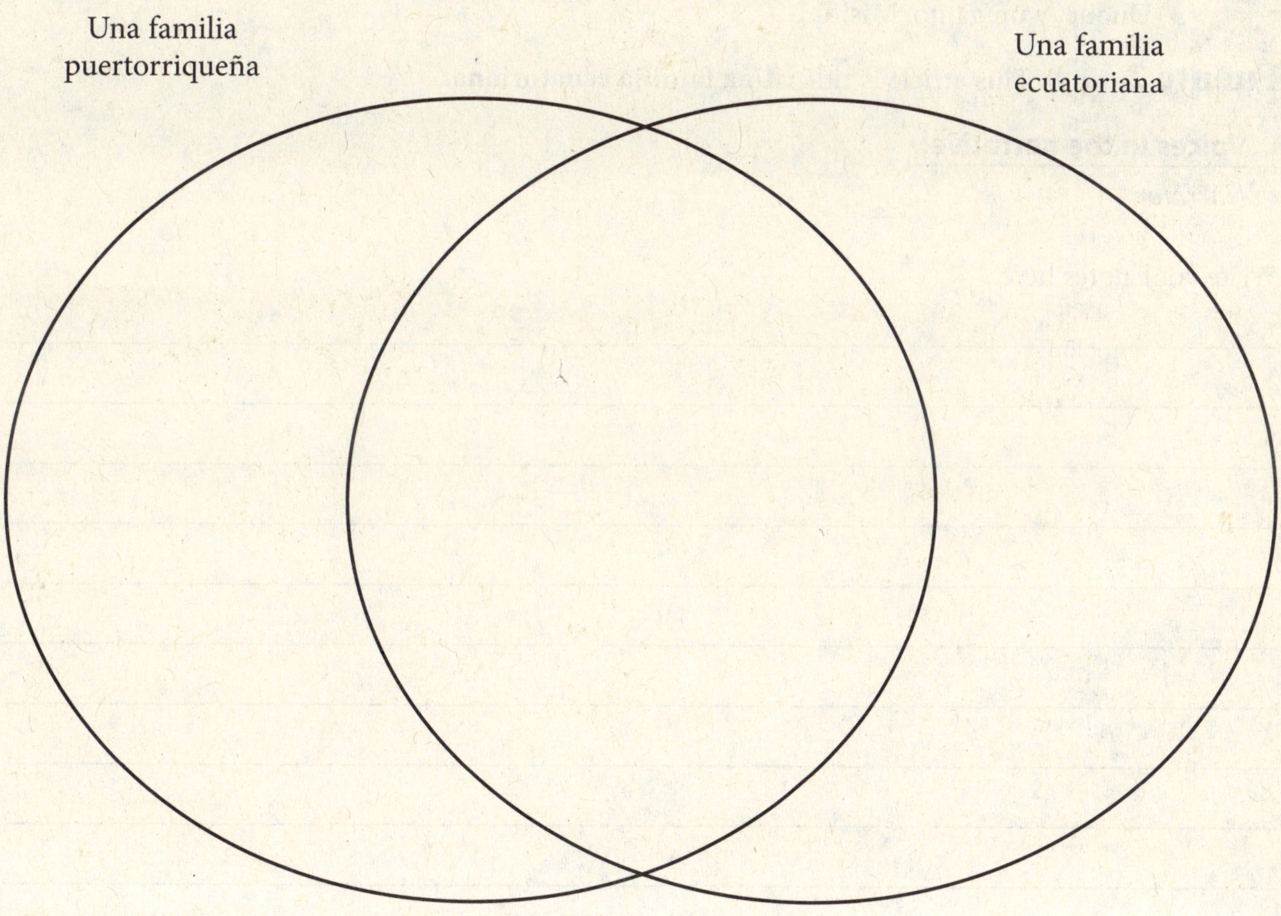

Formal Oral Presentation

Fuente 1 Una familia puertorriqueña

La familia Burgos es de San Juan, la capital de Puerto Rico. En la familia hay siete personas. El padre, la madre, los tres niños—Javier, Teresita y María—y el abuelo y la abuela. Los niños son alumnos en una escuela pública. Son alumnos en la misma escuela porque es una escuela mixta.

Los Burgos tienen una casa muy grande y bonita. La casa tiene seis cuartos y dos baños, una cocina muy grande y dos salas. También, hay un garaje para los automóviles. El jardín es muy bonito y tiene muchas flores muy hermosas de muchos colores vibrantes. Los Burgos también tienen dos mascotas: un perro, Duque, y un gatito, Misifú.

Fuente 2 🎧 This article is titled **Una familia ecuatoriana.**

Voices in the narrative:

Narrator

Write your notes here.

____

____

____

____

____

____

____

____

____

____

____

____

En clase y después

CAPÍTULO ❸ En clase y después ....o

Short Dialogue 

Directions: You will now listen to an audio selection. You may take notes in the space provided. At the end of the selection, you will be asked some questions about what you have just heard. Select the best answer to each question from among the four choices printed in your booklet.

This dialogue is a phone conversation between two classmates, Jorge and Mercedes.

Voices in the dialogue:

Narrator, Jorge, Mercedes

Write your notes here.

____

____

____

____

____

____

❶
a. Jorge and Mercedes do not know each other very well.
b. Jorge and Mercedes do not get along.
c. Jorge and Mercedes are friends.
d. Jorge and Mercedes are the same age.

❷
a. Jorge wants to invite Mercedes to his house.
b. Mercedes wants Jorge to bring a snack.
c. Leonor cannot go to Jorge's house after school.
d. Mercedes wants to invite Jorge to the get-together at Leonor's house.

❸
a. Jorge
b. Leonor
c. Mercedes
d. los padres de Leonor

❹
a. unos CDs
b. unas meriendas
c. unos libros
d. su computadora

❺
a. antes de las clases
b. durante las clases
c. después de las clases
d. Los muchachos no van a la fiesta.

CAPÍTULO ❸ En clase y después ···○

Short Narrative 🎧

Directions: You will now listen to an audio selection. You may take notes in the space provided. At the end of the selection, you will be asked some questions about what you have just heard. Select the best answer to each question from among the four choices printed in your booklet.

This narrative is about a typical school day.

Voices in the narrative:

Narrator

Write your notes here.

____

____

____

____

____

____

❶
  a. Enseñan y dan exámenes.
  b. Hablan cuando los profesores hablan.
  c. Toman apuntes, prestan atención y toman exámenes.
  d. No sacan notas bajas.

❷
  a. una nota
  b. un examen
  c. un cuaderno
  d. una sala

❸
  a. los alumnos
  b. los profesores
  c. las notas
  d. los apuntes

❹
  a. todos los alumnos
  b. algunos alumnos
  c. otros alumnos
  d. Los alumnos no sacan notas.

CAPÍTULO ❸ En clase y despues

Reading Comprehension

Directions: Read the following passage carefully for comprehension. The passage is followed by a number of incomplete statements or questions. Select the completion or answer that is best according to the passage.

This reading is about two high school students from Spain.

La apertura de clases[1]

Es septiembre y en España es el mes de la apertura de clases. Magalí es alumna en una escuela privada en Córdoba—el Colegio de la Trinidad. Magalí lleva uniforme a la escuela y necesita un uniforme nuevo.

En la tienda de ropa Magalí busca una blusa blanca, una falda gris y una chaqueta azul. Es el uniforme obligatorio para su colegio. En total el uniforme cuesta 185 euros. No es barato. La mamá de Magalí paga. Ella paga en la caja.

José Luis es alumno en un colegio público de Madrid. Los alumnos llevan uniforme a su escuela también, pero él no necesita otro uniforme. Él usa la misma talla[2] que el año pasado. José necesita materiales escolares. En la tienda él compra papel, lápices, un bolígrafo, dos cuadernos y cuatro carpetas.

[1]La apertura de clases *Beginning of the school year*
[2]talla *size*

❶ Based on information in the reading, what do we know about the type of currency used in Spain?

a. The currency is called a "barato."

b. The currency is called a "euro."

c. The currency is called a "dólar."

d. No type of currency is mentioned in the reading.

❷ Based on information in the reading, what conclusion can be made about high schools in Spain?

a. All high schools in Spain are private.

b. All high schools in Spain are public.

c. Students at both public and private high schools wear uniforms.

d. The high schools in Spain are very expensive.

❸ ¿Por qué no compra otro uniforme José Luis?

a. Usa la misma talla que el año pasado.

b. No lleva uniforme a la escuela.

c. El uniforme no es barato.

d. Necesita materiales escolares.

❹ El papel, lápiz, bolígrafo y cuaderno son...

a. uniformes.

b. clases.

c. materiales escolares.

d. baratos.

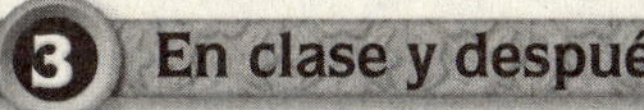

Paragraph Completion (with root words)

Directions: Read the following passage. Then write, on the line after each number, the form of the word in parentheses needed to complete the passage correctly, logically, and grammatically. Be sure to spell and accent the word correctly. You may have to use more than one word in some cases, but you must use a form of the word given in parentheses. Be sure to write the word on the line even if no change is needed.

¡Qué tal! Yo ____1____ en la escuela, en ____2____ clase de español. Si yo ____3____ una pregunta, (yo) ____4____ con mi profesora. Para la escuela, yo ____5____ una mochila, un cuaderno, ____6____ lápices y una carpeta. Después de la escuela, (yo) ____7____ a la tienda para comprar los materiales ____8____. Yo busco ____9____ materiales y ____10____ en la caja.

1. ____________________ (estar)
2. ____________________ (el)
3. ____________________ (tener)
4. ____________________ (hablar)
5. ____________________ (necesitar)
6. ____________________ (un)
7. ____________________ (ir)
8. ____________________ (escolar)
9. ____________________ (el)
10. ____________________ (pagar)

Hoy, en la clase de español ____1____ profesor ____2____ un examen. ____3____ amiga, María, ____4____ una nota ____5____. Ella ____6____ mucho. Ella siempre ____7____ la mano y también contesta muchas ____8____. Después de la escuela, ella y yo ____9____ a la biblioteca con ____10____ amigos y navegamos la red.

1. ____________________ (el)
2. ____________________ (dar)
3. ____________________ (mi)
4. ____________________ (sacar)
5. ____________________ (bueno)
6. ____________________ (estudiar)
7. ____________________ (levantar)
8. ____________________ (pregunta)
9. ____________________ (ir)
10. ____________________ (nuestro)

Paragraph Completion (without root words)

Directions: First read the passage and then write, on the line after each number, an appropriate word to complete the passage correctly, logically, and grammatically. Be sure to spell and accent the word correctly. Only ONE Spanish word should be inserted. You will have to use nouns, articles, adjectives, verbs, etc.

Yo ____1____ a la tienda de ropa y busco un uniforme para ____2____ escuela. Yo compro ____3____ falda azul y una blusa blanca. En ____4____ países hispanohablantes, los alumnos ____5____ uniforme a la escuela.

1. _______________________________

2. _______________________________

3. _______________________________

4. _______________________________

5. _______________________________

PRE-AP WORKBOOK

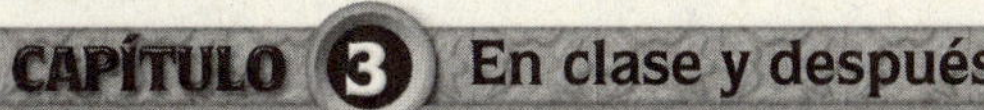

Informal Writing

Directions: For the following question, you will write a message. Your response should be at least 25 words in length.

You are writing an e-mail to your classmate who was not in school the first day. You are informing her about what went on in Spanish class and what school supplies she needs to buy. You may want to:

- tell her who the teacher is

- describe what the teacher is like

- tell her what school supplies she needs

Formal Writing

Directions: The following question is based on the Sources (**Fuentes**) 1–3. The first two sources are readings. Fill in the graphic organizer when you have finished reading them. You will hear audio material for the third source. Take notes as you listen. Then you will plan your response to the question. Your response should be at least 25 words in length.

¿Por qué son famosas las personas de los artículos?

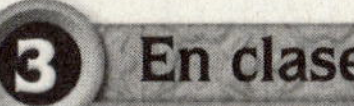

Formal Writing

Fuente 1 Gabriela Mistral

Gabriela Mistral es una poeta famosa. Es de Vicuña. Vicuña es un pequeño pueblo rural de Chile. De joven[1], Gabriela Mistral enseña en varias escuelas primarias en áreas rurales de Chile. Ella pasa unos años como directora de una escuela en Punta Arenas, en el extremo sur de la Patagonia chilena. Hoy la escuela lleva el nombre de la maestra y poeta—el Liceo Gabriela Mistral. Es una maestra excelente y es también una poeta excelente. Como poeta, Gabriela Mistral recibe un gran honor. Gana[2] el Premio Nobel de Literatura.

---

[1]De joven   *As a young woman*
[2]Gana   *She wins*

Formal Writing

Fuente 2 Roberto Clemente

Roberto Clemente es de Carolina, Puerto Rico. Cuando tiene solo diecisiete años ya es jugador[1] profesional de béisbol en Estados Unidos. Cuatro veces es campeón de los bateadores. Gana otros premios también.

Roberto Clemente es también una persona muy buena. Él organiza ayuda[2] para sus hermanos nicaragüenses cuando hay un terremoto[3] horrible en Managua, la capital de Nicaragua.

Hoy hay un gran centro deportivo para los jóvenes de Puerto Rico que lleva el nombre de Roberto Clemente. Hay escuelas en Estados Unidos que llevan su nombre también.

[1]jugador *player*
[2]ayuda *help*
[3]terremoto *earthquake*

Gabriela Mistral es famosa porque...	Roberto Clemente es famoso porque...

Formal Writing

Fuente 3 🎧 The following article is about the famous clothes designer Oscar de la Renta.

Voices in the narrative:

Narrator

Write your notes here.

____

____

____

____

____

____

____

____

____

____

____

____

____

____

____

____

____

____

____

CAPÍTULO ③ En clase y después

Informal Speaking 🎧

Directions: You will participate in a simulated conversation. First, read the outline of the conversation. You will have 20 seconds to respond to each question. Once the conversation begins, a tone will indicate when you should begin and end speaking. You should participate in the conversation as fully and appropriately as possible.

You get a phone call from an international company who is surveying teenagers about school and after school life. You are being interviewed by Mr. Duarte who will ask you several questions.

La conversación The shaded lines reflect what you will be hearing on the recording.

Sr. Duarte:	Greets you.
Tú:	Greet him.
Sr. Duarte:	Asks you a question about school.
Tú:	Answer him.
Sr. Duarte:	Asks you a question about school.
Tú:	Answer him.
Sr. Duarte:	Asks you a question about school.
Tú:	Answer him.
Sr. Duarte:	Asks you a question about your teacher.
Tú:	Answer him.
Sr. Duarte:	Asks you a question about after school activities.
Tú:	Answer him.
Sr. Duarte:	Thanks you and says good-bye.
Tú:	Say good-bye.

Formal Oral Presentation

Directions: The following question is based on the accompanying printed article and audio selection. First, you will read the article. Then, you will hear the audio selection. You should take notes while you listen. You will then respond to the statement below ORALLY.

How does your school compare with the schools discussed in the sources?

Formal Oral Presentation

Fuente 1 Un alumno madrileño

Julio Torres es de Madrid. Él es alumno en el Liceo Joaquín Turina en Madrid. Un liceo o colegio es una escuela secundaria en España. En Madrid, la apertura de clases es a fines de septiembre. Julio necesita muchas cosas para la apertura de clases. Necesita materiales escolares. En una papelería compra un libro, un bolígrafo, tres lápices y varios cuadernos.

Pero Julio no necesita ropa nueva para la escuela. ¿Por qué? Porque Julio no lleva un blue jean o una camiseta a la escuela. Él lleva un uniforme. Es obligatorio llevar uniforme a la escuela. Un muchacho lleva un pantalón negro y una camisa blanca. En algunas escuelas es necesario llevar chaqueta y corbata también. Una muchacha lleva una falda y una blusa. Y a veces es necesario llevar una chaqueta.

Fuente 2 🎧 This article is titled **Escuelas del mundo hispano.**

Voices in the narrative:

Narrator

Write your notes here.

____

____

____

____

____

____

____

____

____

____

____

____

____

¿Qué comemos y dónde?

CAPÍTULO ④ ¿Qué comemos y dónde? ······················○

Short Dialogue 🎧

This dialogue takes place on the terrace of a café.

Voices in the dialogue:

Narrator, Julia, Carlos, Waiter

Write your notes here.

____

____

____

____

____

____

1
  a. impolite
  b. very friendly
  c. polite
  d. tense

2
  a. No hay mucha gente en el café.
  b. Julia y Carlos tienen mucha hambre.
  c. Julia y Carlos no tienen sed.
  d. Julia y Carlos solo desean algo para beber.

3
  a. Hay mucha gente en el café.
  b. No hay muchas mesas ocupadas.
  c. Hay muchos meseros en el café.
  d. Los amigos no ven una mesa libre.

4
  a. Julia
  b. Carlos
  c. el mesero
  d. Isabel

5
  a. aburrida
  b. excelente
  c. graciosa
  d. mala

CAPÍTULO 4 ¿Qué comemos y dónde? ·······················○

Short Narrative 🎧

> **Directions:** You will now listen to an audio selection. You may take notes in the space provided. At the end of the selection, you will be asked some questions about what you have just heard. Select the best answer to each question from among the four choices printed in your booklet.

This narrative is about the importance of family and godparents in Hispanic countries.

Voices in the narrative:

Narrator

Write your notes here.

____

____

____

____

____

____

1   a. al padre y a la madre
    b. a los padres y a los abuelos
    c. a todos los miembros de la familia
    d. a los miembros de la familia y a sus amigos

2   a. Una familia hispana típica es pequeña.
    b. La familia es una unidad importante en la sociedad hispana.
    c. Las fiestas en los países hispanos son muy grandes porque las familias son grandes.
    d. Los padrinos asisten al bebé durante el bautizo.

3   a. países
    b. celebraciones
    c. parientes
    d. sociedades

4   a. todos los parientes y los padrinos
    b. solo los padrinos
    c. solo los padres y los hermanos
    d. No hay fiestas familiares en los países hispanos.

5   a. padrino
    b. unidad
    c. fiesta
    d. familiar

CAPÍTULO 4 ¿Qué comemos y dónde?

Reading Comprehension

Directions: Read the following passage carefully for comprehension. The passage is followed by a number of incomplete statements or questions. Select the completion or answer that is best according to the passage.

Read the dialogue between two friends.

Pablo: Linda, ¿lees el menú en español?

Linda: ¡Sí, claro!

Pablo: Pero, ¿comprendes un menú en español?

Linda: Sí, comprendo. ¿Por qué preguntas?

Pablo: Pero no eres española. Y no vives aquí en Madrid. ¿Lees el español? ¿Cómo es posible?

Linda: Pues, aprendo el español en la escuela en Nueva York. En clase hablamos mucho. Leemos y escribimos también.

Pablo: Pues, yo aprendo el inglés aquí en Madrid. Hablo un poco, pero cuando leo no comprendo casi nada. Comprendo muy poco.

1 ¿Dónde están los amigos?

a. en la escuela

b. en un café

c. en casa

d. en una tienda

2 ¿De dónde es Linda?

a. de Madrid

b. del café

c. de Nueva York

d. del sur de España

3 ¿Cuáles son las actividades en que participa Linda en su clase de español?

a. Lee, habla y escribe en español.

b. Lee, habla y escribe en inglés.

c. Lee el menú en español.

d. No comprende casi nada.

4 ¿Quién habla un poco de inglés?

a. Linda

b. Pablo

c. el mesero

d. el profesor de inglés

5 ¿De qué nacionalidad es Pablo?

a. español

b. estadounidense

c. inglés

d. norteamericano

CAPÍTULO 4 ¿Qué comemos y dónde? .... o

Paragraph Completion (with root words)

Directions: Read the following passage. Then write, on the line after each number, the form of the word in parentheses needed to complete the passage correctly, logically, and grammatically. Be sure to spell and accent the word correctly. You may have to use more than one word in some cases, but you must use a form of the word given in parentheses. Be sure to write the word on the line even if no change is needed.

Cada día nosotros ____1____ el desayuno, el almuerzo y la cena. Para el desayuno, yo ____2____ pan tostado con dos huevos antes de ir a ____3____ escuela. Para el almuerzo, mis amigos y yo ____4____ a la cafetería de la escuela. Tomamos un bocadillo, ____5____ ensalada o una hamburguesa con papas fritas. Después de la escuela, como la cena en casa con ____6____ familia. Mi madre ____7____ una cena ____8____. Mi comida favorita ____9____ arroz con pollo. ¡Voy a ____10____ ahora!

1. __________________________ (tomar)
2. __________________________ (comer)
3. __________________________ (el)
4. __________________________ (ir)
5. __________________________ (un)
6. __________________________ (mi)
7. __________________________ (preparar)
8. __________________________ (delicioso)
9. __________________________ (ser)
10. __________________________ (comer)

Hoy ____1____ viernes y nosotros ____2____ a cenar con ____3____ amigos. Nosotros ____4____ en un restaurante puertorriqueño. El nombre de ____5____ restaurante es «Las Palmas». Estamos aquí porque nosotros ____6____ comer comida de la isla de Puerto Rico—arroz y frijoles, pollo, tostones y ensalada mixta. Nosotros esperamos ____7____ comida. Acabamos de ____8____ con la mesera. Por fin, cuando llegan los platos, saboreamos los sabores ____9____ de nuestra isla favorita. ¡Es ____10____ experiencia increíble!

1. __________________________ (ser)
2. __________________________ (ir)
3. __________________________ (nuestro)
4. __________________________ (estar)
5. __________________________ (el)
6. __________________________ (desear)
7. __________________________ (el)
8. __________________________ (hablar)
9. __________________________ (diferente)
10. __________________________ (un)

CAPÍTULO ❹ ¿Qué comemos y dónde? ·· o

Paragraph Completion (without root words)

Directions: First read the passage and then write, on the line after each number, an appropriate word to complete the passage correctly, logically, and grammatically. Be sure to spell and accent the word correctly. Only ONE Spanish word should be inserted. You will have to use nouns, articles, adjectives, verbs, etc.

Nosotros acabamos _____1_____ llegar _____2_____ restaurante más famoso de la ciudad. Tenemos _____3_____ hablar con el mesero. Hay muchas opciones en _____4_____ menú. Hay pizza, ensaladas, hamburguesas, bocadillos y mucho más. Decidimos comer _____5_____ hamburguesas con papas fritas.

1. _________________________________

2. _________________________________

3. _________________________________

4. _________________________________

5. _________________________________

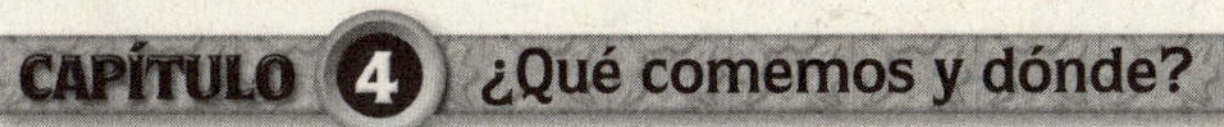

Informal Writing

Directions: For the following question, you will write a message. Your response should be at least 30 words in length.

You are writing an e-mail to your key pal and he has asked you to describe your eating habits. You may want to tell him:

- what your favorite meal is
- when and what you typically eat during the day
- what your favorite restaurant is
- when you go to the restaurant
- what you order when you go

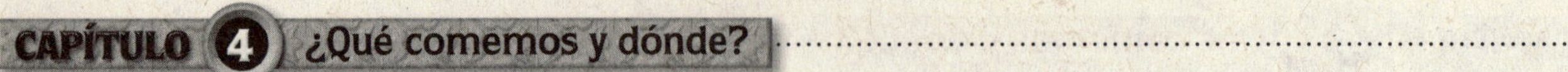

CAPÍTULO ④ ¿Qué comemos y dónde?

Formal Writing

Directions: The following question is based on the Sources (**Fuentes**) 1–3. The first two sources are readings. You will hear audio material for the third source. Take notes as you listen. Then you will plan your response to the statement or question below. Your response should be at least 40 words in length.

Describe un café típico en España o Latinoamérica. ¿Quiénes van a un café? ¿Adónde vas tú para tomar una merienda y hablar con tus amigos? ¿Qué comes o bebes?

CAPÍTULO 4 ¿Qué comemos y dónde? ···o

Formal Writing

Fuente 1 Una merienda ¿Dónde?

En un café

Después de las clases en España y Latinoamérica muchos alumnos van a un café o una cafetería. Muchos cafés tienen una terraza al aire libre[1]. Cuando hace buen tiempo buscan una mesa libre en la terraza.

En el café toman un refresco si solo desean beber algo o toman una merienda si desean comer algo. En el café ven a sus amigos y conversan con ellos. Hablan de muchas cosas.

En un mesón

Los universitarios van a un mesón. Los mesones son muy populares en España pero hay mesones en Latinoamérica también. En el mesón los estudiantes hablan con sus amigos y comen tapas en España o antojitos en Latinoamérica. No tienen que leer un menú porque ven los antojitos o tapas en platos en una barra y seleccionan los antojitos que desean comer.

Los tunos

A veces entra en el mesón un grupo de tunos. Los tunos son músicos que tocan[2] la guitarra y cantan[3]. Los estudiantes cantan con ellos. Los tunos son populares sobre todo en España y en Guanajuato, México.

----

[1]al aire libre *outdoor*
[2]tocan *play*
[3]cantan *sing*

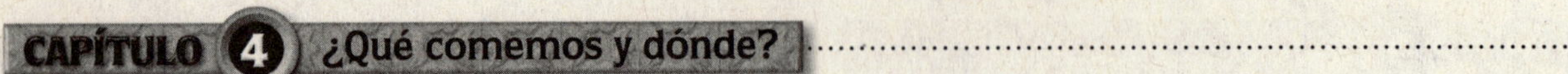

Formal Writing

Fuente 2 El almuerzo en un café

Son las doce menos diez. Manuel y Carlos van a un café para tomar el almuerzo. Carlos tiene mucho calor y también tiene mucha sed. Por eso, tiene que beber algo. Manuel también desea algo de beber. Buscan una mesa en la terraza. Tienen hambre y deciden comer algunas tapas también. Para beber, Carlos toma una cola bien fría. Manuel toma un agua mineral. Con sus bebidas, comen albóndigas, empanadas y tostones. Manuel y Carlos saborean todo. ¡Mmm, qué rico!

CAPÍTULO 4 ¿Qué comemos y dónde?

Formal Writing

Fuente 3 🎧 The following narrative is titled **En un café en Madrid**.

Voices in the narrative:

Narrator

Write your notes here.

____

____

____

____

____

____

____

____

____

____

____

____

____

____

____

____

____

____

____

Informal Speaking 🎧

Directions: You will participate in a simulated conversation. First, read the outline of the conversation. You will have 20 seconds to respond to each question. Once the conversation begins, a tone will indicate when you should begin and end speaking. You should participate in the conversation as fully and appropriately as possible.

Imagine you are having a conversation with Ana, your friend from Colombia. She will ask you some questions about your eating habits.

La conversación The shaded lines reflect what you will be hearing on the recording.

Ana: Greets you.

Tú: Greet her.

Ana: Asks you a question about breakfast.

Tú: Answer her.

Ana: Asks you another question about breakfast.

Tú: Answer her.

Ana: Asks you a question about lunch.

Tú: Answer her.

Ana: Asks you another question about lunch.

Tú: Answer her.

Ana: Asks you a question about dinner.

Tú: Answer her.

Ana: Asks you another question about dinner.

Tú: Answer her.

CAPÍTULO 4 ¿Qué comemos y dónde?

Formal Oral Presentation

Directions: The following question is based on the accompanying printed article and audio selection. First, you will read the article. Then, you will hear the audio selection. You should take notes while you listen. You will then respond to the statement below ORALLY.

How do your eating habits compare to the ones mentioned in the sources?

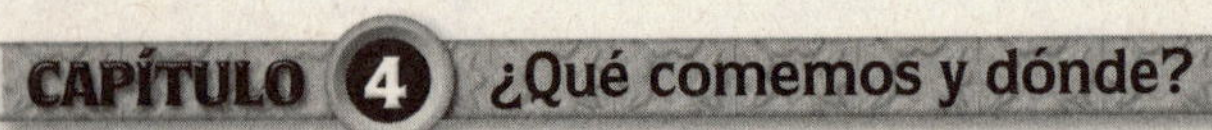

Formal Oral Presentation

Fuente 1 Las horas para comer

El desayuno

En España y en los países de Latinoamérica, la gente suele[1] comer más tarde que aquí en Estados Unidos. Como nosotros, toman el desayuno a eso de las siete o las ocho de la mañana. A eso de las diez van a un café o a una cafetería donde toman otro café con leche y un churro o pan dulce.

El almuerzo

El almuerzo es a la una o, en el caso de España, a eso de las dos de la tarde. Hoy día la mayoría[2] de la gente no va a casa a tomar el almuerzo. Toman el almuerzo en la cafetería de la escuela o en la cafetería donde trabajan. Si no, comen en un café o en un restaurante. Muchos no van a casa a tomar el almuerzo porque hay mucho tráfico. Tarda (Toma) demasiado tiempo.[3]

La cena

En la mayoría de los países latinoamericanos la gente suele cenar a las ocho y media o a las nueve de la noche. Pero, en España, no. En España la cena es a las diez o a las diez y media.

---

[1]suele *tend to*
[2]mayoría *majority*
[3]demasiado tiempo *too much time*

Fuente 2 This article is titled **La comida en otras partes.**

Voices in the narrative:

Narrator

Write your notes here.

	el desayuno	el almuerzo	la cena
España			
Nicaragua			

Deportes

Short Dialogue 🎧

The following is a conversation between two friends.

Voices in the dialogue:

Anita, Tomás

Write your notes here.

____

____

____

____

____

____

1
a. de las clases
b. de sus familias
c. de los deportes
d. del juego

2
a. el béisbol
b. el fútbol
c. el tenis
d. el baloncesto

3
a. ser espectador
b. ser jugador
c. ser campeón
d. This information is not given in the conversation.

4
a. muy bueno
b. campeonatos
c. malo
d. This information is not given in the conversation.

5
a. Tomás thinks his team will lose.
b. There is no championship this year.
c. The team has already won the championship.
d. The team has not yet won the championship, but Tomás thinks they will.

CAPÍTULO ⑤ Deportes ....o

Short Narrative 🎧

Directions: You will now listen to an audio selection. You may take notes in the space provided. At the end of the selection, you will be asked some questions about what you have just heard. Select the best answer to each question from among the four choices printed in your booklet.

You will hear a sports broadcast on a Spanish radio station.

Voices in the narrative:

Broadcaster

Write your notes here.

____

____

____

____

____

____

❶
a. el fútbol
b. el béisbol
c. el baloncesto
d. el tenis

❷
a. dos horas
b. el segundo tiempo
c. muy poco tiempo
d. No queda tiempo.

❸
a. el Real Madrid y Vargas
b. el Real Madrid y el Barcelona
c. el Barcelona y Vargas
d. el Balón y Vargas

❹
a. Vargas
b. el portero de Madrid
c. el portero de Barcelona
d. el espectador

❺
a. Su equipo gana.
b. Su equipo pierde.
c. El Real Madrid pierde.
d. No tienen equipo.

Reading Comprehension

Directions: Read the following passage carefully for comprehension. The passage is followed by a number of incomplete statements or questions. Select the completion or answer that is best according to the passage.

This reading is about famous archeological sites in Latin America that reveal information about sports and games in pre-Columbian cultures.

Honduras y México

En Copán en Honduras y en Chichén Itzá en México hay ruinas de varias canchas de pelota. La cancha en Copán data de 775 después de Cristo. Es interesante notar que los juegos de los mayas de Copán y los juegos de los mayas de Chichén Itzá son bastante similares. Los indios usan una pelota grande de goma[1] y no pueden tocar la pelota con las manos. El juego es una diversión pero en Chichén Itzá tiene también sentido religioso. Después del juego sacrifican a los jugadores que ganan.

Puerto Rico

Hay una famosa excavación arqueológica cerca de Ponce en Puerto Rico. ¿Y qué descubren? Descubren una cancha de pelota. Y el juego que juegan los indios taínos de Puerto Rico es parecido o similar al juego de los mayas de Centroamérica. El juego de los taínos es el batú. El batú es un juego de diversión pero tiene también sentido religioso. En el juego hay dos bandos o equipos. Juegan con una pelota de goma. Uno de los bandos lanza la pelota al otro bando. El otro bando

[1]goma   *rubber*

tiene que devolver la pelota. Y no pueden usar las manos. Tienen que lanzar la pelota con la pierna, la rodilla, o el brazo pero no pueden tocar la pelota con la mano. El equipo que deja rodar[2] la pelota por el suelo[3] el mayor número de veces[4] pierde el juego.

[2]deja rodar   *lets roll*
[3]suelo   *ground*
[4]mayor número de veces   *greatest number of times*

1 ¿Dónde están las ruinas arqueológicas en Honduras?

   a. Chichén Itzá

   b. Ponce

   c. Copán

   d. Puerto Rico

2 ¿En qué país está Chichén Itzá?

   a. Puerto Rico

   b. Honduras

   c. Ponce

   d. México

3 ¿Cómo es similar el juego de los taínos al juego de los mayas?

   a. No puedes tocar la pelota con las manos.

   b. Sacrifican a los jugadores que ganan.

   c. No puedes dejar rodar la pelota en el suelo.

   d. No puedes tocar la pelota con la cabeza.

4 ¿Qué juegan los indios de Puerto Rico?

   a. el taíno

   b. la pelota

   c. el batú

   d. la diversión

5 If you were participating in the ball game at Chichén Itzá, why would you not necessarily want to be on the winning team?

   a. The players on the winning team are given a trophy.

   b. The players on the winning team are sacrificed.

   c. The players on the winning team are not allowed to use their hands.

   d. The players on the losing team are given a trophy.

CAPÍTULO 5 Deportes ···o

Paragraph Completion (with root words)

Directions: Read the following passage. Then write, on the line after each number, the form of the word in parentheses needed to complete the passage correctly, logically, and grammatically. Be sure to spell and accent the word correctly. You may have to use more than one word in some cases, but you must use a form of the word given in parentheses. Be sure to write the word on the line even if no change is needed.

A mí me _____1_____ mucho _____2_____ al béisbol. Mi amigo juega también. Nosotros _____3_____ jugadores en un equipo de béisbol. Durante el juego, todos _____4_____ jugadores _____5_____ batear un jonrón. _____6_____ materiales que nosotros _____7_____ para el juego son: una pelota, un bate, un guante, un platillo y tres bases. _____8_____ equipo es bueno, pero (nosotros) no _____9_____ ganar siempre. A veces perdemos. Pero todos los partidos son _____10_____.

1. _________________________ (gustar)

2. _________________________ (jugar)

3. _________________________ (ser)

4. _________________________ (el)

5. _________________________ (querer)

6. _________________________ (Un)

7. _________________________ (necesitar)

8. _________________________ (Nuestro)

9. _________________________ (poder)

10. _________________________ (divertido)

Diego _____1_____ el alumno más atlético de su escuela. Él _____2_____ tres deportes diferentes. En el otoño, juega a _____3_____ fútbol. Diego es el capitán de _____4_____ equipo. Cuando _____5_____ la pelota casi siempre marca un tanto. ¡GOL! En el invierno, Diego es un miembro de _____6_____ equipo de baloncesto. Dribla con el balón en la cancha y los espectadores _____7_____. Diego y su equipo ganan _____8_____ partidos. En la primavera, Diego juega al béisbol. Es un cátcher _____9_____. Siempre atrapa _____10_____ pelota.

1. _________________________ (ser)

2. _________________________ (jugar)

3. _________________________ (el)

4. _________________________ (su)

5. _________________________ (lanzar)

6. _________________________ (el)

7. _________________________ (aplaudir)

8. _________________________ (mucho)

9. _________________________ (fantástico)

10. _________________________ (el)

Paragraph Completion (without root words)

Directions: First read the passage and then write, on the line after each number, an appropriate word to complete the passage correctly, logically, and grammatically. Be sure to spell and accent the word correctly. Only ONE Spanish word should be inserted. You will have to use nouns, articles, adjectives, verbs, etc.

Hoy ____1____ el primer juego de béisbol de Juan. Toda ____2____ familia ____3____ a ir a mirar el partido en ____4____ estadio de la escuela. ____5____ muchas personas en el estadio. El juego ____6____ a las tres y media ____7____ la tarde y termina a las cinco ____8____ media.

1. _______________________

2. _______________________

3. _______________________

4. _______________________

5. _______________________

6. _______________________

7. _______________________

8. _______________________

Informal Writing

Directions: For the following question, you will write a message. Your response should be at least 25 words in length.

You are writing an e-mail to your key pal from Panama. He has asked you to describe your favorite team uniform or T-shirt. Tell him what your favorite team uniform or T-shirt is. You may want to include:

- the name of the team
- what sport they play
- what the uniform or T-shirt is like
- what the colors are
- why you like the team

Formal Writing

Directions: The following question is based on the Sources (**Fuentes**) 1–3. The first two sources are readings. Fill in the graphic organizer when you have finished reading them. You will hear audio material for the third source. Take notes as you listen. Then you will plan your response to the question. Your response should be at least 40 words in length.

How does your favorite athlete compare with the ones mentioned?

Formal Writing

Fuente 1 Una estrella de golf

De origen mexicanoamericano, una atleta que gana fama mundial es Nancy López. ¿Cuál es su deporte? Su deporte es el golf. Nancy López es una de las estrellas más brillantes del golf mundial. Ella empieza a practicar el golf cuando todavía es muy joven. Cuando tiene solo doce años recibe su primer premio del Campeonato Junior de Chicas en 1972. Ella gana otra vez en 1974. Nancy va a la Universidad de Tulsa y juega golf con su equipo. En la universidad ella gana el titulo *All American*. En su primer viaje en el torneo LPGA, ella gana nueve veces en los torneos más difíciles en el área profesional norteamericana. También, gana el título de «la Jugadora del Año» por cuatro años. Cuando tiene treinta años Nancy es miembro del salón de la fama de golf.

CAPÍTULO 5 Deportes ···○

Formal Writing

Fuente 2 Un atleta estupendo

John Martínez es de Nueva York, pero sus padres son de la República Dominicana. De joven, John empieza a practicar deportes. Cuando John tiene solo quince años ya es un atleta estupendo. Pero John no practica el béisbol ni tampoco el fútbol. Él practica el deporte de pista y campo[1] en su escuela. Él gana muchas carreras[2] y ahora asiste a la Universidad de Nueva York. Él forma parte del equipo universitario. Los corredores del equipo de la universidad son muy buenos. John también participa en los Juegos Panamericanos Junior en 2005 en Canadá. En los Juegos Panamericanos participan atletas de todos los países de las Américas.

[1]pista y campo   *track and field*
[2]carreras   *races*

Nancy López	John Martínez

Formal Writing

Fuente 3 🎧 This narrative gives information about the famous athlete Ricardo (Pancho) González.

Voices in the narrative:

Narrator

Write your notes here.

____

____

____

____

____

____

____

____

____

____

____

____

____

____

____

____

____

____

Informal Speaking 🎧

> **Directions:** You will participate in a simulated conversation. First, read the outline of the conversation. You will have 20 seconds to respond to each question. Once the conversation begins, a tone will indicate when you should begin and end speaking. You should participate in the conversation as fully and appropriately as possible.

Imagine you are talking to your friend from Colombia, Luisa. She is asking you questions about sports in your school.

La conversación The shaded lines reflect what you will be hearing on the recording.

Luisa:	Greets you.
Tú:	Greet her.
Luisa:	Asks you a question about school sports.
Tú:	Answer her.
Luisa:	Asks you another question about school sports.
Tú:	Answer her.
Luisa:	Asks you a question about the school uniform.
Tú:	Answer her.
Luisa:	Asks you a question about the games.
Tú:	Answer her.
Luisa:	Asks you another question about the games.
Tú:	Answer her.
Luisa:	Asks you a final question.
Tú:	Answer her.

Formal Oral Presentation

Directions: The following question is based on the accompanying printed article and audio selection. First, you will read the article. Then, you will hear the audio selection. You should take notes while you listen. You will then respond to the statement below ORALLY.

Compare the two sports mentioned in the sources. Which of the two do you prefer to play or watch? You may want to use the graphic organizer below to organize your thoughts.

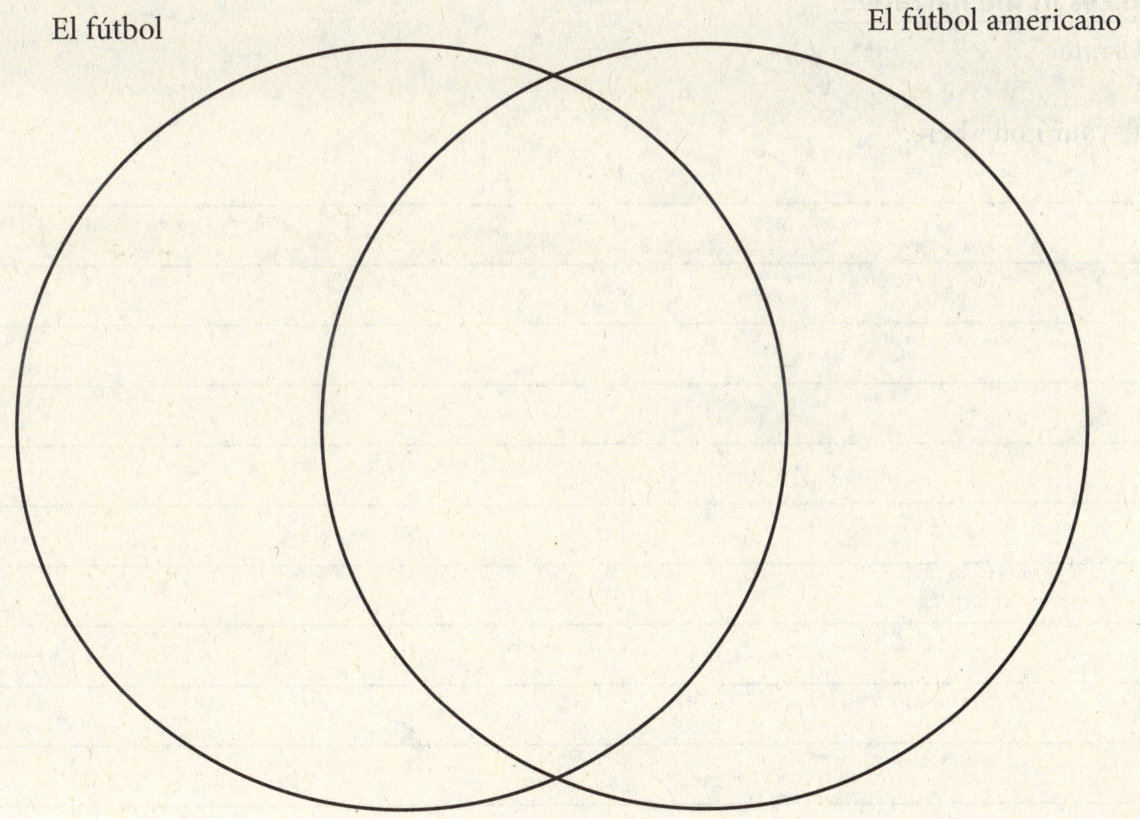

Formal Oral Presentation

Fuente 1 El fútbol americano

Un deporte muy popular en Estados Unidos es el fútbol americano. Es más popular que el béisbol. Treinta y dos equipos forman la liga profesional, la Liga Nacional de Fútbol o *National Football League (NFL)*. Es una liga muy popular. Muchas personas van a los estadios para mirar los partidos de fútbol americano.

El *Super Bowl* es el partido final de la temporada en donde los dos mejores equipos de la liga juegan para el trofeo. De todos los equipos de fútbol americano solo dos equipos pueden jugar en el *Super Bowl*.

Fuente 2 🎧 The narrative is titled **El fútbol.**

Voices in the narrative:

Narrator

Write your notes here.

____

____

____

____

____

____

____

____

____

____

____

____

El bienestar

CAPÍTULO 6 — El bienestar

Short Dialogue 🎧

Directions: You will now listen to an audio selection. You may take notes in the space provided. At the end of the selection, you will be asked some questions about what you have just heard. Select the best answer to each question from among the four choices printed in your booklet.

This dialogue takes place in a doctor's office.

Voices in the dialogue:

Narrator, Alejandro, Doctor López

Write your notes here.

____

____

____

____

____

1
a. Está bien.
b. Solo necesita un examen físico.
c. Está enfermo.
d. Necesita comprar unos medicamentos.

2
a. fiebre
b. dolor de cabeza
c. dolor de garganta
d. all of the above

3
a. sus síntomas
b. su receta
c. la boca
d. la garganta

4
a. que Alejandro tiene algo serio
b. que el médico tiene antibióticos
c. que Alejandro no tiene nada serio
d. que Alejandro tiene que ir a clase

5
a. guardar cama
b. jugar fútbol
c. tomar antibióticos
d. ir a la farmacia

Short Narrative 

Directions: You will now listen to an audio selection. You may take notes in the space provided. At the end of the selection, you will be asked some questions about what you have just heard. Select the best answer to each question from among the four choices printed in your booklet.

This narrative is about pharmacies and medicines in Spanish-speaking countries.

Voices in the narrative:

Narrator

Write your notes here.

____

____

____

____

1.
a. No hay farmacias en Estados Unidos.
b. Los farmacéuticos te dan una receta.
c. Los médicos te dan antibióticos.
d. Necesitas una receta de un médico para comprar antibióticos.

2.
a. el farmacéutico
b. el paciente
c. la farmacia
d. la receta

3.
a. un antibiótico
b. todo tipo de medicamento
c. un medicamento que contiene alcohol
d. un medicamento que cuesta mucho

4.
a. Porque no necesitas una receta.
b. Porque los farmacéuticos despachan antibióticos.
c. Porque las farmacias son más grandes.
d. This information is not given in the narrative.

5.
a. Pharmacists in the U.S. cannot sell antibiotics without a prescription.
b. Medicines cost more in Spanish-speaking countries.
c. Pharmacists in Spanish-speaking countries cannot sell antibiotics without a prescription.
d. Doctors in the United States cannot prescribe medicines that contain alcohol.

Reading Comprehension

Directions: Read the following passage carefully for comprehension. The passage is followed by a number of incomplete statements or questions. Select the completion or answer that is best according to the passage.

This reading is about how to stay healthy by eating a balanced diet.

Comer bien

Es muy importante comer bien para mantener la salud. Cada día debemos comer una variedad de vegetales, frutas, granos y cereales y carnes o pescado.

Las proteínas son especialmente importantes durante los períodos de crecimiento[1]. Los adolescentes, por ejemplo, deben comer comestibles o alimentos ricos[2] en proteínas.

Los carbohidratos son alimentos como los espaguetis, las papas y el arroz. Los carbohidratos te dan mucha energía.

Las grasas[3] o lípidos también te dan energía. Algunas carnes contienen mucha grasa. Pero es necesario controlar el consumo de lípidos o grasa porque en muchos individuos elevan el nivel del colesterol.

Las vitaminas son indispensables para el funcionamiento del organismo o cuerpo.

[1]períodos de crecimiento   *growth periods*
[2]ricos   *rich*
[3]grasas   *fats*

1 ¿Por qué deben comer los adolescentes alimentos que contienen mucha proteína?

a. Los adolescentes tienen muchos períodos de crecimiento.

b. Los adolescentes necesitan comer muchos granos.

c. Los adolescentes no deben comer mucha grasa.

d. Es necesario controlar el consumo de frutas y vegetales.

2 ¿Cuál es la idea principal de la lectura?

a. Las frutas y los vegetales son importantes porque contienen vitaminas.

b. Si quieres tener más energía, debes comer muchos carbohidratos.

c. Algunas carnes contienen mucha grasa.

d. Es importante comer bien para mantener la salud.

3 ¿Cuál de los siguientes alimentos no es un carbohidrato?

a. el arroz

b. la carne

c. las papas

d. los espaguetis

4 Si tienes un nivel elevado de colesterol, ¿de qué debes controlar el consumo?

a. las frutas

b. los lípidos

c. los carbohidratos

d. las vitaminas

5 The following sentence will be added to the reading. In which paragraph does it belong?

Las frutas y los vegetales contienen muchas vitaminas.

a. first

b. third

c. fourth

d. fifth

CAPÍTULO 6 El bienestar ·······································o

Paragraph Completion (with root words)

Directions: Read the following passage. Then write, on the line after each number, the form of the word in parentheses needed to complete the passage correctly, logically, and grammatically. Be sure to spell and accent the word correctly. You may have to use more than one word in some cases, but you must use a form of the word given in parentheses. Be sure to write the word on the line even if no change is needed.

Yo _____1_____ enferma hoy. Yo _____2_____ dolor de cabeza y también tengo la garganta _____3_____. Tengo que _____4_____ a la consulta del médico. Mi madre _____5_____ muy _____6_____ porque yo estoy muy enferma. En la consulta, yo le explico mis síntomas a _____7_____ médico. El médico me explica que no es nada serio. Pero, necesito _____8_____ cama. Estoy muy contenta porque no tengo que tomar medicina. A mí no me _____9_____ tomar pastillas. Dentro de poco yo _____10_____ a estar bien.

1. _______________________ (estar)

2. _______________________ (tener)

3. _______________________ (rojo)

4. _______________________ (ir)

5. _______________________ (estar)

6. _______________________ (nervioso)

7. _______________________ (el)

8. _______________________ (guardar)

9. _______________________ (gustar)

10. _______________________ (ir)

José y Teresa _____1_____ muy _____2_____ porque acaban de recibir una nota buena en _____3_____ examen de español. Elena está muy triste porque _____4_____ de recibir una nota _____5_____. José y Teresa tienen _____6_____ sonrisa en la cara. La mamá de José también está muy _____7_____. Ella _____8_____ a preparar la comida _____9_____ de José para celebrar la ocasión. José le invita a Teresa a cenar en _____10_____ casa.

1. _______________________ (estar)

2. _______________________ (contento)

3. _______________________ (el)

4. _______________________ (acabar)

5. _______________________ (malo)

6. _______________________ (un)

7. _______________________ (alegre)

8. _______________________ (ir)

9. _______________________ (favorito)

10. _______________________ (su)

CAPÍTULO 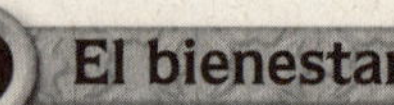 6 El bienestar ···o

Paragraph Completion (without root words)

Directions: First read the passage and then write, on the line after each number, an appropriate word to complete the passage correctly, logically, and grammatically. Be sure to spell and accent the word correctly. Only ONE Spanish word should be inserted. You will have to use nouns, articles, adjectives, verbs, etc.

La muchacha está en ____1____ consulta del médico. Ella ____2____ fiebre y la médica le ____3____ la temperatura y el pulso. Luego, la médica le examina ____4____ garganta. La médica ____5____ da una receta a la pobre muchacha.

1. _______________________

2. _______________________

3. _______________________

4. _______________________

5. _______________________

 **CAPÍTULO 6** El bienestar

Informal Writing

Directions: For the following question, you will write a message. Your response should be at least 30 words in length.

You are not feeling well and you are writing an e-mail to one of your classmates because you will not be in school today. You may want to tell him or her

- why you will not be in school
- how you are feeling
- what your symptoms are
- what you are going to do to feel better

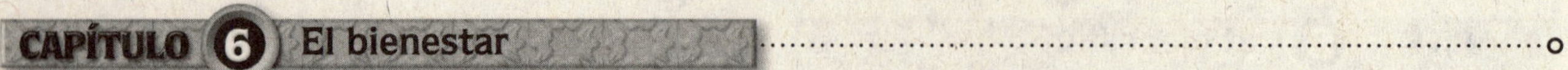

Formal Writing

Directions: The following question is based on the Sources (**Fuentes**) 1–3. The first two sources are readings. Fill in the graphic organizer when you have finished reading them. You will hear audio material for the third source. Take notes as you listen. Then you will plan your response to the question. Your response should be at least 35 words in length.

¿Quién es tu doctor(a)? Compara a tu doctor(a) con los doctores en las fuentes.

CAPÍTULO 6 El bienestar

Formal Writing

Fuente 1 Una biografía—El doctor Antonio Gassett

El doctor Antonio Gassett es de la Habana, Cuba. Recibe su diploma en ciencias en la Universidad de Belén, en Cuba. Más tarde estudia en la Universidad de La Habana. Poco después, sale de Cuba por razones políticas. Va a Boston donde trabaja de técnico de laboratorio en la Fundación de Retina de Boston. Le interesa mucho el trabajo con los ojos y decide estudiar oftalmología. Estudia en Harvard y en la Universidad de la Florida. Hoy el doctor Gassett es una persona famosa. Descubre un método para tratar la cornea. Con el tratamiento del doctor Gassett muchas personas ciegas—que no pueden ver—recobran la vista. El doctor recibe muchos premios por sus investigaciones y descubrimientos.

Formal Writing

Fuente 2 Un ganador del Premio Nobel

Severo Ochoa es de España. Estudia en la Universidad de Madrid. Después de recibir su diploma en medicina, decide que quiere enseñar. Trabaja como profesor en las universidades de Heidelberg y Oxford. En 1940 va a Estados Unidos para trabajar en el departamento de bioquímica en la Universidad de Nueva York. Severo Ochoa y su compañero de trabajo reciben el Premio Nobel en fisiología o medicina en 1959. Sus investigaciones nos ayudan a comprender el metabolismo del cuerpo humano.

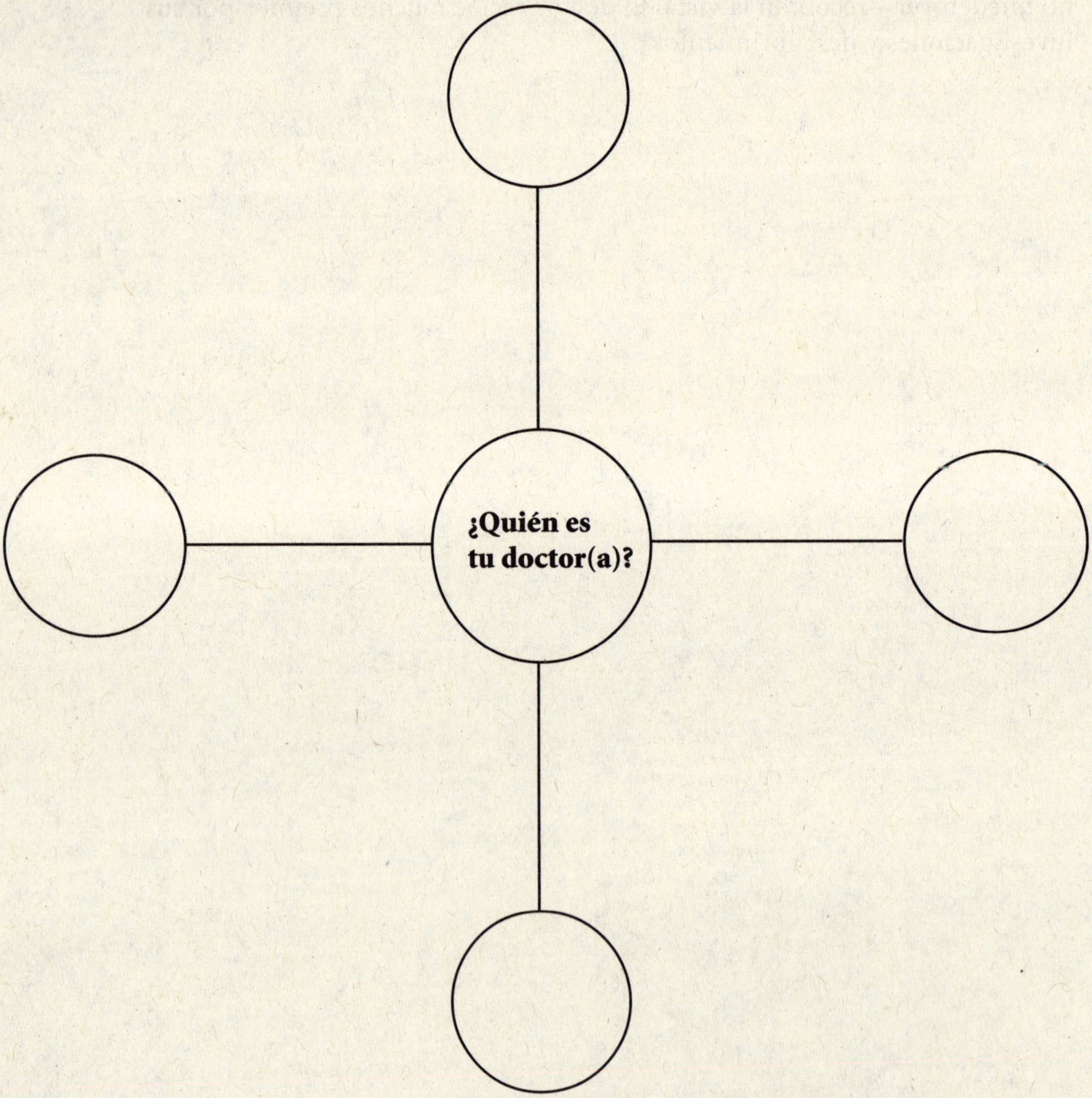

CAPÍTULO 6 El bienestar ·······································○

Formal Writing

Fuente 3 🎧 The following article is about Doctor Antonia Novello.

Voices in the narrative:

Narrator

Write your notes here.

____

____

____

____

____

____

____

____

____

____

____

____

____

____

____

____

____

____

____

____

Informal Speaking 

Directions: You will participate in a simulated conversation. First, read the outline of the conversation. You will have 20 seconds to respond to each question. Once the conversation begins, a tone will indicate when you should begin and end speaking. You should participate in the conversation as fully and appropriately as possible.

You make a phone call to your doctor's office because you are not feeling well and you need to make an appointment.

La conversación The shaded lines reflect what you will be hearing on the recording.

La recepcionista:	Greets you.
Tú:	Greet her.
La recepcionista:	Asks you who is speaking.
Tú:	Give her your name.
La recepcionista:	Asks how she can help you.
Tú:	Tell her you are sick.
La recepcionista:	Asks you about your symptoms.
Tú:	Answer her.
La recepcionista:	Asks you a final question.
Tú:	Answer her.
La recepcionista:	Says good-bye.
Tú:	Say good-bye.

CAPÍTULO ⑥ El bienestar

Formal Oral Presentation

Directions: The following question is based on the accompanying printed article and audio selection. First, you will read the article. Then, you will hear the audio selection. You should take notes while you listen. You will then respond to the statement below ORALLY.

Both of the sources deal with young people who are feeling sick but have made plans to do an activity. Compare and contrast their situations. What do you do when you feel sick but have plans to do something fun?

Formal Oral Presentation

Fuente 1 El pobre paciente de la doctora Rodríguez

Todos sus pacientes quieren mucho a la doctora Rodríguez porque ella es paciente y siempre escucha cuando sus pacientes le explican sus síntomas. Ella tiene también una personalidad energética. Siempre tiene una sonrisa para sus pacientes y siempre está de buen humor.

La doctora Rodríguez está en su oficina. Hoy ella está muy ocupada porque tiene muchos pacientes. Uno de sus pacientes, Roberto, tiene fiebre, dolor de cabeza y la garganta muy roja. Roberto está muy cansado.

La doctora puede ver que Roberto está muy enfermo. Roberto le explica a la doctora Rodríguez que hoy hay una fiesta en casa de su amigo. Roberto quiere ir a la fiesta. Desafortunadamente, la doctora le explica al pobre Roberto que tiene que guardar cama. ¡Él no puede ir a la fiesta! Ahora Roberto no solo está enfermo pero también está triste.

Fuente 2 🎧 This article is titled **Una joven nerviosa.**

Voices in the narrative:

Narrator, Patricia, Doctor

Write your notes here.

____

____

____

____

____

____

____

____

____

____

____

CAPÍTULO 7

De vacaciones

CAPÍTULO 7 De vacaciones

Short Dialogue 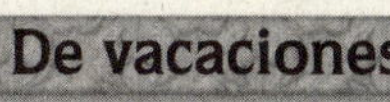

Directions: You will now listen to an audio selection. You may take notes in the space provided. At the end of the selection, you will be asked some questions about what you have just heard. Select the best answer to each question from among the four choices printed in your booklet.

This dialogue is a conversation between two friends, Gloria and Paula.

Voices in the dialogue:

Narrator, Gloria, Paula

Write your notes here.

____

____

____

____

____

1 a. anoche
   b. hoy
   c. la semana pasada
   d. ayer

2 a. Nadó en el mar.
   b. Tomó el sol.
   c. Jugó voleibol.
   d. Practicó la plancha de vela.

3 a. con su familia
   b. con Gloria
   c. con sus amigos
   d. This information is not in the dialogue.

4 a. Paula fue a la playa.
   b. Paula lo pasó muy bien.
   c. Paula nadó en su blue jean.
   d. Paula no puede nadar.

5 a. seria
   b. graciosa
   c. muy organizada
   d. antipática

Short Narrative 🎧

Directions: You will now listen to an audio selection. You may take notes in the space provided. At the end of the selection, you will be asked some questions about what you have just heard. Select the best answer to each question from among the four choices printed in your booklet.

The following is a radio announcement.

Voices in the narrative:

Announcer

Write your notes here.

____

____

____

____

____

____

1
a. un viaje a la playa
b. un viaje a una estación de esquí
c. unas clases de esquiar
d. ropa y equipaje para esquiar

2
a. Gorostiza
b. Bariloche
c. Córdoba
d. Buenos Aires

3
a. Gorostiza
b. Bariloche
c. Córdoba
d. Buenos Aires

4
a. expertos
b. principiantes
c. expertos y principiantes
d. No hay clases.

5
a. alto
b. incluido
c. bajo
d. fabuloso

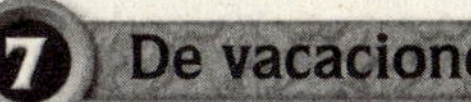

CAPÍTULO 7 De vacaciones ⋯⋯⋯⋯⋯⋯⋯⋯⋯⋯⋯⋯⋯⋯⋯⋯⋯⋯⋯⋯⋯o

Reading Comprehension

Directions: Read the following passage carefully for comprehension. The passage is followed by a number of incomplete statements or questions. Select the completion or answer that is best according to the passage.

This reading is about weather and climate.

El clima y el tiempo

El clima y el tiempo son dos cosas muy diferentes. El tiempo es la condición de la atmósfera durante un período breve o corto. El tiempo puede cambiar[1] frecuentemente. Puede cambiar varias veces en un solo día.

El clima es el término que usamos para el tiempo que prevalece[2] en una zona por un período largo. El clima es el tiempo que hace cada año en el mismo lugar.

Zonas climáticas

En el mundo de habla española hay muchas zonas climáticas. Mucha gente cree que toda la América Latina tiene un clima tropical, pero es erróneo. El clima de Latinoamérica varía de una región a otra.

El Amazonas

Toda la zona o cuenca amazónica es una región tropical. Hace mucho calor y llueve mucho durante todo el año.

Los Andes

En los Andes, aun en las regiones cerca de la línea ecuatorial[3], el clima no es tropical. En las zonas montañosas el clima depende de la elevación. En los picos andinos, por ejemplo, hace frío.

Clima templado

Algunas partes de Argentina, Uruguay y Chile tienen un clima templado. España también tiene un clima templado. En una región de clima templado hay cuatro estaciones: el verano, el otoño, el invierno y la primavera. Y el tiempo cambia con cada estación. ¡Y una cosa importante! Las estaciones en la América del Sur son inversas de las de la América del Norte.

⋯⋯⋯⋯⋯⋯⋯⋯⋯⋯⋯⋯⋯⋯⋯⋯⋯⋯⋯⋯⋯

[1]cambiar   *change*
[2]prevalece   *prevails*
[3]línea ecuatorial   *equator*

 El tiempo...

   a. es similar al clima.

   b. puede cambiar mucho.

   c. no cambia.

   d. es un término que usamos para describir el clima durante un período largo.

 ¿Cómo es un clima tropical?

   a. Es caloroso y llueve mucho.

   b. Es caloroso y no hay mucha lluvia.

   c. Hace frío y hay mucha nieve.

   d. Hay cuatro estaciones.

3 ¿Por qué hace frío en algunas regiones cerca de la línea ecuatorial?

  a. Hay nieve en los picos andinos.

  b. El clima cambia con las estaciones.

  c. El clima depende de la elevación.

  d. Es una región tropical.

4 Basado en la lectura, ¿qué tiempo hace en Chile en enero?

  a. Hace frío.

  b. Hace calor.

  c. Es otoño.

  d. Hay mucha nieve.

CAPÍTULO 7 De vacaciones ···○

Paragraph Completion (with root words)

Directions: Read the following passage. Then write, on the line after each number, the form of the word in parentheses needed to complete the passage correctly, logically, and grammatically. Be sure to spell and accent the word correctly. You may have to use more than one word in some cases, but you must use a form of the word given in parentheses. Be sure to write the word on the line even if no change is needed

Estamos de vacaciones en un balneario en Mallorca, España. Es verano y ___1___ mucho calor y mucho sol. Mi familia y yo ___2___ a la playa ayer. Todos ___3___ traje de baño, anteojos de sol y sandalias. Toda la familia jugó al voleibol en ___4___ cancha de voleibol con la familia de Luis. Las dos familias ___5___ bien. Y, ¿quién ___6___ el partido? Pues, todos ganaron. Los muchachos ___7___ el balón varias veces y el balón pasó por encima de ___8___ red y los dos equipos marcaron tantos. Cansados de jugar y con mucha hambre, nosotros fuimos a ___9___. Pasamos una tarde muy ___10___.

1. __________________________ (hacer)

2. __________________________ (ir)

3. __________________________ (llevar)

4. __________________________ (el)

5. __________________________ (jugar)

6. __________________________ (ganar)

7. __________________________ (golpear)

8. __________________________ (el)

9. __________________________ (comer)

10. __________________________ (agradable)

Julio y ___1___ amigos ___2___ a patinar sobre el hielo ayer. Para patinar sobre el hielo, los patinadores, o ___3___ personas que patinan, llevan patines. Julio y sus amigos fueron a ___4___ pista al aire libre. Para no tener frío, ellos ___5___ un gorro en la cabeza y guantes en ___6___ manos. Los amigos ___7___ a una pista de patinaje muy ___8___. Es el «Centro de Rockefeller» en la Ciudad de Nueva York. Allí van muchas personas cada año durante la temporada de Navidad para patinar debajo de ___9___ árbol ___10___.

1. __________________________ (su)

2. __________________________ (ir)

3. __________________________ (el)

4. __________________________ (un)

5. __________________________ (llevar)

6. __________________________ (el)

7. __________________________ (ir)

8. __________________________ (famoso)

9. __________________________ (el)

10. __________________________ (navideño)

Paragraph Completion (without root words)

Directions: First read the passage and then write, on the line after each number, an appropriate word to complete the passage correctly, logically, and grammatically. Be sure to spell and accent the word correctly. Only ONE Spanish word should be inserted. You will have to use nouns, articles, adjectives, verbs, etc.

Estamos en ____1____ estación de esquí. Todos (nosotros) llevamos chaqueta, guantes y botas porque ____2____ mucho frío. También hay mucha nieve en ____3____ montañas. Los amigos van a esquiar. ¿Qué ____4____ que hacer? Tienen que comprar ____5____ tickets para ____6____ telesquí. Los compran en la ventanilla.

1. _______________________________
2. _______________________________
3. _______________________________
4. _______________________________
5. _______________________________
6. _______________________________

Informal Writing

Directions: For the following question, you will write a message. Your response should be at least 35 words in length.

You are on vacation in a resort in Argentina. You write an e-mail to your friend. You may want to tell him or her

- what the weather is like
- where you are staying
- with whom you are on vacation
- what activities you are enjoying

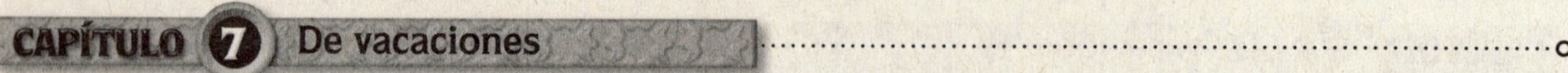

CAPÍTULO 7 De vacaciones

Formal Writing

Directions: The following question is based on the Sources (**Fuentes**) 1–3. The first two sources are readings. Fill in the graphic organizer when you have finished reading them. You will hear audio material for the third source. Take notes as you listen. Then you will plan your response to the question. Your response should be at least 25 words in length.

Compare and contrast how each of the three students spent their vacations. How do you like to spend your vacation?

Formal Writing

Fuente 1 En la Costa del Sol

Diego y su familia pasaron todo el mes de agosto en Estepona, en la famosa Costa del Sol en el sur de España. Ellos son de Madrid. Llegaron a Estepona después de un viaje de unas ocho horas.

A Diego le gustó mucho Estepona. Pasó muchos días en la playa donde nadó y tomó el sol. A veces fue con su familia a un chiringuito, un tipo de café o restaurante en la playa. En el chiringuito almorzaron. A Diego le gustaron mucho el pescado y los mariscos del Mediterráneo.

Un día fueron a Tarifa. Diego lo pasó bien en Tarifa donde practicó la plancha de vela y el surfing. Tarifa es un lugar ideal para la plancha de vela porque casi siempre hace viento y el mar está bastante bravo. Hay olas grandes que les encantan a todos los surfistas.

Formal Writing

Fuente 2 Las vacaciones de Sarita

Sarita es una joven puertorriqueña. Ella vive en San Juan, la capital de Puerto Rico. San Juan está en la costa y tiene playas bonitas. Siempre hace calor. El verano es eterno. Por eso, Sarita no tiene que visitar otra ciudad cuando quiere pasar sus vacaciones en un balneario.

El mes pasado pasó una semana en un hotel con la familia de su amiga Sandra. Fueron a una playa privada. Los papás de Sandra alquilaron un barquito y las amigas esquiaron en el agua. Sandra esquió muy bien. También, jugaron al voleibol con otros jóvenes en la playa. Tomaron muchas fotos que les van a mostrar a sus amigos cuando empiezan las clases.

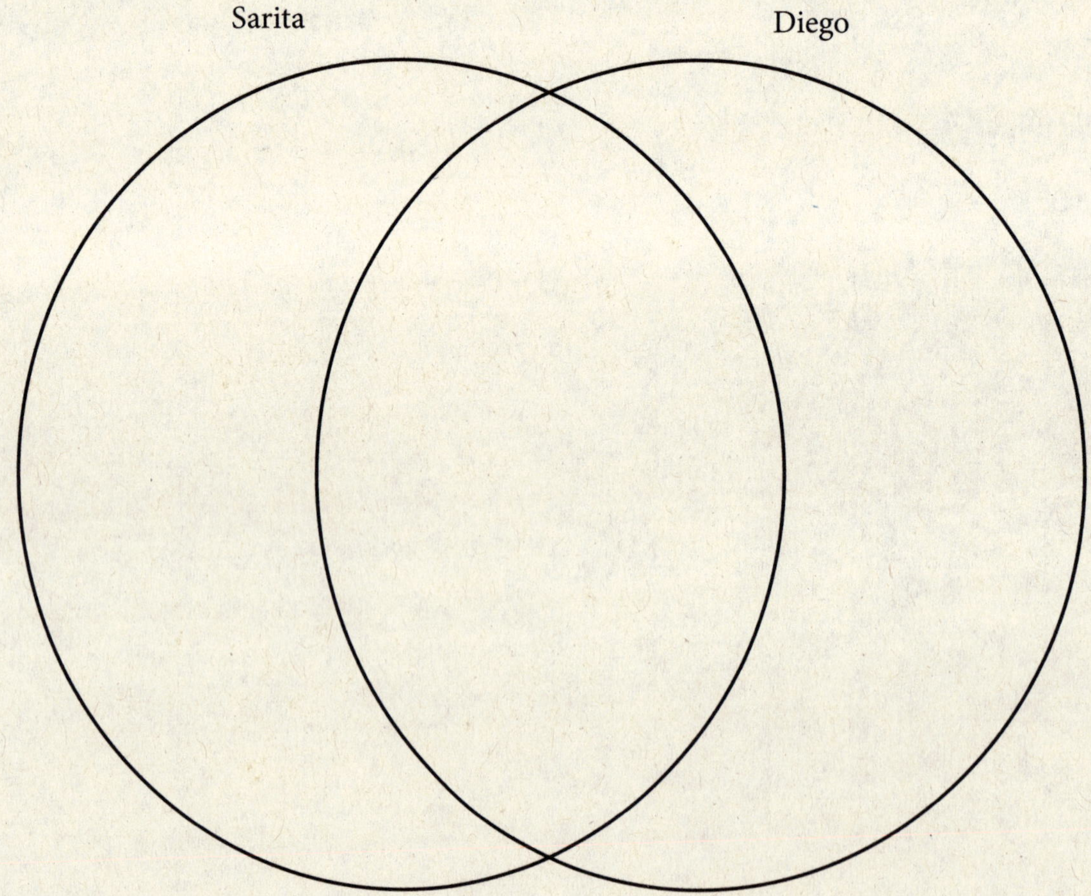

CAPÍTULO 7 De vacaciones

Formal Writing

Fuente 3 🎧 The following article is titled **Julio en Argentina.**

Voices in the narrative:

Narrator

Write your notes here.

____

____

____

____

____

____

____

____

____

____

____

____

____

____

____

____

____

____

____

CAPÍTULO ⑦ De vacaciones ·································○

Informal Speaking 🎧

Directions: You will participate in a simulated conversation. First, read the outline of the conversation. You will have 20 seconds to respond to each question. Once the conversation begins, a tone will indicate when you should begin and end speaking. You should participate in the conversation as fully and appropriately as possible.

You receive a phone call from an international travel agency telling you that you have just won a vacation to a Spanish-speaking country. This person needs details from you to make arrangements.

La conversación The shaded lines reflect what you will be hearing on the recording.

El agente:	He greets you.
Tú:	Greet him.
El agente:	He tells you the good news.
Tú:	You reply.
El agente:	He asks you a question about the trip.
Tú:	Answer him.
El agente:	He asks you another question about the trip.
Tú:	Answer him.
El agente:	He asks you a final question.
Tú:	Answer him.
El agente:	He thanks you and says good-bye.
Tú:	Thank him and say good-bye.

CAPÍTULO 7 De vacaciones

Formal Oral Presentation

Directions: The following question is based on the accompanying printed article and audio selection. First, you will read the article. Then, you will hear the audio selection. You should take notes while you listen. You will then respond to the statement or question below ORALLY.

¿Por qué son importantes las playas en los países hispanos? ¿En qué actividades participamos en la playa?

CAPÍTULO ⑦ De vacaciones ···○

Formal Oral Presentation

Fuente 1 Paraísos del mundo hispano

¿Viajar por el mundo hispano y no pasar unos días en un balneario? ¡Qué lástima! En los países de habla española hay playas fantásticas. España, Puerto Rico, Cuba, la República Dominicana, México, Uruguay—todos son países famosos por sus playas.

En el verano cuando hace calor y un sol bonito brilla en el cielo, ¡qué estupendo es pasar un día en la playa! Y en lugares (sitios) como México, Puerto Rico y Venezuela el verano es eterno. Podemos ir a la playa durante todos los meses del año.

Muchas personas toman sus vacaciones en una playa donde pueden disfrutar de su tiempo libre. En la playa nadan o toman el sol. Pero, ¡cuidado! Es necesario usar una crema solar porque el sol es muy fuerte en las playas tropicales.

Fuente 2 🎧 This article is titled **Un día en una playa de España.**

Voices in the narrative:

Narrator

Write your notes here.

____

____

____

____

____

____

____

____

____

En tu tiempo libre

CAPÍTULO 8 En tu tiempo libre

Short Dialogue 🎧

Directions: You will now listen to an audio selection. You may take notes in the space provided. At the end of the selection, you will be asked some questions about what you have just heard. Select the best answer to each question from among the four choices printed in your booklet.

This dialogue is a telephone conversation between two friends, Paco and Julia.

Voices in the dialogue:

Paco, Julia

Write your notes here.

____

____

____

____

1
a. Paco
b. Felipe
c. su mamá
d. Nadie la llamó.

2
a. No escuchó su móvil.
b. No volvió a casa hasta las ocho y media.
c. Salió con su familia.
d. Habló con su mamá.

3
a. Felipe y Paco
b. Julia y Paco
c. Julia y Felipe
d. Felipe y su familia

4
a. a la sesión de las ocho y media
b. a la sesión de las diez
c. a la sesión de las cinco
d. a la sesión de las siete

5
a. Julia was not hungry when she arrived home.
b. Julia ate dinner at her house before she went out.
c. Julia and Paco are not very good friends.
d. Paco went out last night, too.

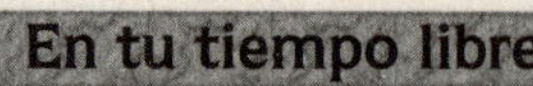

CAPÍTULO 8 En tu tiempo libre ⋯⋯⋯⋯⋯⋯⋯⋯⋯⋯⋯⋯⋯⋯⋯⋯⋯⋯○

Short Narrative 

> **Directions:** You will now listen to an audio selection. You may take notes in the space provided. At the end of the selection, you will be asked some questions about what you have just heard. Select the best answer to each question from among the four choices printed in your booklet.

The following is a radio announcement.

Voices in the narrative:

Announcer

Write your notes here.

____

____

____

____

____

1
  a. de un concierto
  b. de una exposición de arte
  c. de una película
  d. de una exposición de baile

2
  a. anoche
  b. la semana pasada
  c. el año pasado
  d. hoy por la mañana

3
  a. emocionante y tierna
  b. famosa y fabulosa
  c. emocionante y triste
  d. tranquila y contenta

4
  a. el nombre del personaje principal
  b. el actor
  c. el niño
  d. el director

5
  a. una
  b. dos
  c. tres
  d. cuatro

CAPÍTULO **8** En tu tiempo libre

Reading Comprehension

Directions: Read the following passage carefully for comprehension. The passage is followed by a number of incomplete statements or questions. Select the completion or answer that is best according to the passage.

This article is titled *Dating*.

Algunas diferencias culturales son muy interesantes. Y las diferencias culturales pueden tener una influencia en la lengua que hablamos. Por ejemplo, *dating, boyfriend* y *girlfriend* son palabras que usamos mucho en inglés, ¿no? Y son palabras que no tienen equivalente exacto en español. ¿Cómo es posible? Pues, vamos a hablar con Verónica. Ella es de Perú.

—Verónica, ¿saliste anoche?

—Sí, salí con un grupo de amigos de la escuela.

—¿Adónde fueron?

—Fuimos al cine. Vimos una película muy buena. Fue una película americana. La vimos en versión original con subtítulos en español.

—Verónica, ¿no sales a veces sola con un muchacho, con un amigo de la escuela?

—Pues, no mucho. Generalmente salimos en grupo. Pero es algo que está cambiando[1]. Hoy en día una pareja[2] joven puede salir a solas. Podemos ir a un café, por ejemplo, a tomar un refresco. A veces vamos al cine o solo damos un paseo[3] por el parque. Pero, para nosotros, es algo bastante nuevo.

[1]cambiando *changing*
[2]pareja *couple*
[3]damos un paseo *take a walk*

1 ¿Cuál es la idea principal del artículo?

a. No hay palabras en español que significan *dating, boyfriend* y *girlfriend*.

b. Hay diferencias culturales en las costumbres de *dating* entre los jóvenes norteamericanos y los de países hispanohablantes.

c. No hay diferencias en las costumbres de *dating* entre los jóvenes norteamericanos y los de países hispanohablantes.

d. Muchas costumbres están cambiando en los países hispanohablantes.

2 ¿De qué país habla específicamente el artículo?

a. de Perú

b. de Ecuador

c. de Colombia

d. de todos los países latinoamericanos

3 Generalmente, ¿con quién sale Verónica?

a. Ella sale con un grupo de amigos.

b. Ella sale con un muchacho de la escuela.

c. Ella sale con solo amigas.

d. Ella sale con su familia.

4 Según el artículo, ¿en cuál de las siguientes actividades NO participan las parejas jóvenes?

a. dar un paseo

b. ir a un café

c. ir de vacaciones

d. ir al cine

CAPÍTULO 8 En tu tiempo libre

Paragraph Completion (with root words)

Directions: Read the following passage. Then write, on the line after each number, the form of the word in parentheses needed to complete the passage correctly, logically, and grammatically. Be sure to spell and accent the word correctly. You may have to use more than one word in some cases, but you must use a form of the word given in parentheses. Be sure to write the word on the line even if no change is needed.

Ayer ____1____ el cumpleaños de Anita. Para ____2____ la ocasión su familia le ____3____ una fiesta muy linda. Ella invitó a ____4____ gente. A ____5____ celebración asistieron todos sus familiares y compañeros del colegio. ____6____ abuelos le ____7____ una torta muy ____8____. Todos los invitados ____9____ mucho— carne, arroz y varias tapas. A todos ____10____ gustó la fiesta.

1. _________________________ (ser)
2. _________________________ (celebrar)
3. _________________________ (dar)
4. _________________________ (mucho)
5. _________________________ (el)
6. _________________________ (Su)
7. _________________________ (preparar)
8. _________________________ (rico)
9. _________________________ (comer)
10. _________________________ (le)

Unos amigos ____1____ al museo la semana ____2____. Ellos ____3____ una exposición de arte contemporáneo. En un salón admiraron ____4____ cuadros del pintor famoso Salvador Dalí. El pintor ____5____ de origen español. En otro salón admiraron cuadros de una famosa pintora ____6____, Frida Khalo. Muchos de ____7____ cuadros son autorretratos. Son de ella misma. Los amigos ____8____ que hay ____9____ artistas de habla hispana que ____10____ fama mundial.

1. _________________________ (ir)
2. _________________________ (pasado)
3. _________________________ (ver)
4. _________________________ (un)
5. _________________________ (ser)
6. _________________________ (mexicano)
7. _________________________ (su)
8. _________________________ (aprender)
9. _________________________ (mucho)
10. _________________________ (tener)

Paragraph Completion (without root words)

Directions: First read the passage and then write, on the line after each number, an appropriate word to complete the passage correctly, logically, and grammatically. Be sure to spell and accent the word correctly. Only ONE Spanish word should be inserted. You will have to use nouns, articles, adjectives, verbs, etc.

Mi amiga y yo _____1_____ a un concierto de Marc Anthony anoche. El concierto fue en Madison Square Garden en _____2_____ Ciudad de Nueva York. Nosotros pagamos $75 por _____3_____ entradas. _____4_____ banda de Marc Anthony es muy talentosa. Marc Anthony también _____5_____ un cantante con mucho talento.

1. _______________________

2. _______________________

3. _______________________

4. _______________________

5. _______________________

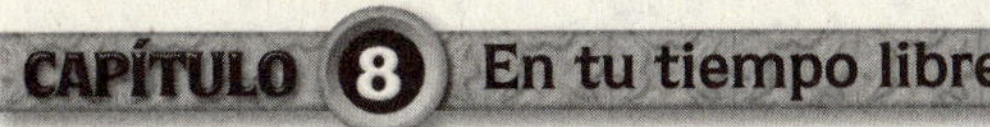

CAPÍTULO 8 En tu tiempo libre

Informal Writing

Directions: For the following question, you will write a message. Your response should be at least 35 words in length.

You are writing an e-mail to your friend in which you are describing a trip to a museum. You may want to include

- what museum you visited
- when you went
- with whom you went
- what you saw
- what you liked about the trip

Formal Writing

Directions: The following question is based on the Sources (**Fuentes**) 1–3. The first two sources are readings. You will hear audio material for the third source. Take notes as you listen. Then you will plan your response to the question. Your response should be at least 40 words in length.

¿Por qué es importante asistir a eventos culturales como los que son mencionados en las fuentes? ¿Cuál de los siguientes eventos te interesa más? ¿Por qué?

Formal Writing

Fuente 1 El baile

El Ballet Folklórico de México goza de fama mundial. El espectáculo que presenta el Ballet Folklórico todos los domingos y miércoles en el Palacio de Bellas Artes es uno de los shows más populares de la Ciudad de México. La compañía baila una variedad de danzas regionales de México. A veces la coreografía del Ballet Folklórico de México es muy graciosa y divertida.

Hay también el Ballet Folklórico Nacional de México. Esta compañía presenta un programa auténtico y clásico de danzas mexicanas regionales en el Teatro de la Ciudad.

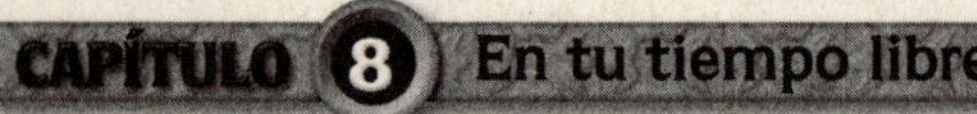

Formal Writing

Fuente 2 El flamenco andaluz

El flamenco andaluz es de origen oriental, árabe y gitano. Es muy popular en Andalucía, región de mucha influencia mora[1] y gitana en el sur de España. Las canciones apasionantes del flamenco salen del alma. Hay dos grupos de cantes—el cante chico y el cante jondo. Los cantos del cante chico son más ligeros[2] y alegres. Los del cante jondo tratan del amor, de la muerte y de todo el drama humano. El tono es optimista o pesimista, alegre o triste, como la vida misma.

El baile flamenco es tan apasionante como el canto. El baile va acompañado de la guitarra, palmadas[3], castañuelas y los espontáneos «olés» de los espectadores.

---

[1]mora *Moorish*
[2]ligeros *light*
[3]palmadas *claps*

CAPÍTULO (8) En tu tiempo libre

Formal Writing

Fuente 3 🎧 The following article is titled **La zarzuela.**

Write your notes here.

____

____

____

____

____

____

____

____

____

____

____

____

____

____

____

____

____

____

____

____

Informal Speaking 🎧

Directions: You will participate in a simulated conversation. First, read the outline of the conversation. You will have 20 seconds to respond to each question. Once the conversation begins, a tone will indicate when you should begin and end speaking. You should participate in the conversation as fully and appropriately as possible.

You receive a phone call from your friend Miguel. He wants to know all about your evening last night.

La conversación The shaded lines reflect what you will be hearing on the recording.

Miguel:	Te saluda.
Tú:	Le saludas.
Miguel:	Te pregunta sobre la película.
Tú:	Le contestas.
Miguel:	Te pregunta sobre la película.
Tú:	Le contestas.
Miguel:	Te pregunta sobre el precio de los boletos.
Tú:	Le contestas.
Miguel:	Te pregunta sobre la película.
Tú:	Le contestas.
Miguel:	Te pregunta sobre la película.
Tú:	Le contestas.

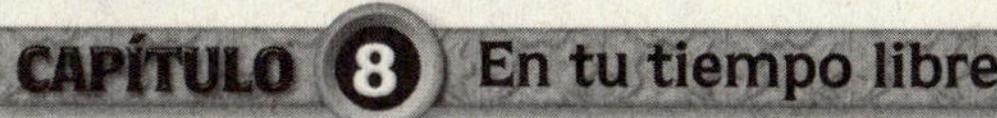

CAPÍTULO 8 En tu tiempo libre

Formal Oral Presentation

Directions: The following question is based on the accompanying printed article and audio selection. First, you will read the article. Then, you will hear the audio selection. You should take notes while you listen. You will then respond to the statement or question below ORALLY.

What are the similarities and differences between the cultural activities mentioned in the sources and the cultural activities in which you participate?

Formal Oral Presentation

Fuente 1 Un día de cultura hispana en la escuela

El año pasado los alumnos de español en nuestra escuela participaron en una excursión muy interesante. Fueron con los profesores a una escuela intermedia. Hablaron con los alumnos de la escuela intermedia y les explicaron que el estudio de una lengua extranjera puede ser divertido. ¿Cómo puede ser divertido? Pues, los alumnos dieron presentaciones para demostrar la importancia de aprender lenguajes extranjeros y lo divertido que es. Les enseñaron canciones en español y bailes famosos del mundo hispanohablante. A los estudiantes de las escuelas intermedias les gustaron mucho las presentaciones. ¿Por qué? Porque fue un día divertido de cultura hispana. Después de las presentaciones todos los estudiantes fueron a un típico restaurante mexicano. Todos pasaron un día muy agradable.

Fuente 2 This article is titled **Domingo, día 18 de febrero.**

Voices in the narrative:

Narrator

Write your notes here.

____

____

____

____

____

____

____

____

____

¡Vamos de compras!

CAPÍTULO 9 ¡Vamos de compras!

Short Dialogue 🎧

Directions: You will now listen to an audio selection. You may take notes in the space provided. At the end of the selection, you will be asked some questions about what you have just heard. Select the best answer to each question from among the four choices printed in your booklet.

This dialogue is a conversation between two friends, Ana and Casandra.

Voices in the dialogue:

Ana, Casandra

Write your notes here.

____

____

____

____

____

____

1
  a. en casa
  b. en un mercado indígena
  c. en una tienda de ropa
  d. en el supermercado

2
  a. un vestido verde
  b. una blusa verde
  c. una blusa roja
  d. un vestido rojo

3
  a. treinta y seis
  b. treinta y tres
  c. veintitrés
  d. Ella no sabe qué talla usa.

4
  a. su amiga
  b. su mamá
  c. la dependienta
  d. la vendedora del puesto

CAPÍTULO ❾ ¡Vamos de compras! ·· o

Short Narrative 🎧

The following is an announcement.

Voices in the narrative:

Announcer

Write your notes here.

____

____

____

____

____

____

____

❶ a. en una papelería

   b. en un mercado

   c. en una tienda de ropa

   d. en la caja

❷ a. una oferta de camisetas

   b. una liquidación de toda la mercancía

   c. una oferta de blusas

   d. una oferta de pantalones

❸ a. Costaron menos de cincuenta pesos.

   b. Costaron cincuenta pesos.

   c. Costaron más de cincuenta pesos.

   d. Costaron cuarenta y dos pesos.

❹ a. Hay muchos colores y estilos.

   b. Hay muchos colores y precios.

   c. Hay muchas tallas y estilos.

   d. Hay muchas tallas y colores.

Reading Comprehension

Directions: Read the following passage carefully for comprehension. The passage is followed by a number of incomplete statements or questions. Select the completion or answer that is best according to the passage.

This article is titled Mercados al aire libre.

En las ciudades y pueblos de Latinoamérica en donde hay mucha influencia indígena, hay mercado uno o dos días a la semana. La mayoría de estos mercados están al aire libre. La actividad de compra y venta empieza muy temprano por la mañana y todo ya está cerrado a la una de la tarde. Igual que en los mercados municipales hay puestos o tenderetes pero muchos vendedores se sientan en el suelo[1] mismo y exhiben sus productos tendidos sobre una manta[2]. Además de vender comestibles hay puestos de objetos de artesanía tales como platos y tejidos y otras mercancías y provisiones necesarias para el mantenimiento de la casa. Y en los alrededores del mercado hay mucha actividad donde hacen sus negocios[3] los vendedores ambulantes.

[1]suelo *ground*
[2]tendidos sobre una manta *spread out on a blanket*
[3]hacen sus negocios *do business*

1 Muchos mercados indígenas...

  a. empiezan tarde.

  b. ya están cerrados a las nueve de la mañana.

  c. están al aire libre.

  d. están en edificios antiguos.

2 ¿Qué puedes comprar en un mercado indígena?

  a. comestibles, artesanía y mercancía para la casa

  b. solo comestibles

  c. productos frescos y congelados

  d. artesanía y mercancía para la casa

3 Si vas a un mercado indígena, ¿a qué hora debes llegar?

  a. a las dos de la tarde

  b. a la una de la tarde

  c. temprano por la mañana

  d. a las cinco de la tarde

4 ¿Por qué hay mucha actividad en las calles alrededor del mercado?

  a. Hay muchos vendedores ambulantes en los alrededores del mercado.

  b. Dan presentaciones culturales en los alrededores del mercado.

  c. Hay tiendas donde venden mercancías para la casa.

  d. Hay muchos tenderetes en los alrededores del mercado.

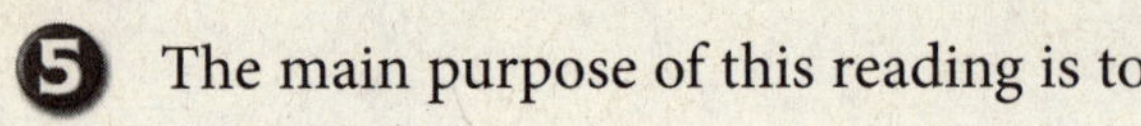

CAPÍTULO 9 ¡Vamos de compras!

5 The main purpose of this reading is to...

a. inform readers about indigenous markets in Spanish-speaking countries.

b. convince readers to buy a product found at an indigenous market.

c. inform readers about a particular indigenous market.

d. persuade readers not to shop at an indigenous market.

CAPÍTULO 9 ¡Vamos de compras!

Paragraph Completion (with root words)

Directions: Read the following passage. Then write, on the line after each number, the form of the word in parentheses needed to complete the passage correctly, logically, and grammatically. Be sure to spell and accent the word correctly. You may have to use more than one word in some cases, but you must use a form of the word given in parentheses. Be sure to write the word on the line even if no change is needed.

Hoy ____1____ domingo. Mi madre y yo ____2____ que ir de compras. Vamos a ____3____ un regalo para mi abuelita que cumple ochenta años ____4____ próxima semana.

Yo ____5____ que a mi abuelita le ____6____ las joyas y antigüedades. Nosotros ____7____ a visitar la Feria de Antigüedades en el barrio de San Telmo. Yo quiero mucho a ____8____ abuelita. Su fiesta va a ser la fiesta más ____9____ del pueblo porque todos ____10____ quieren mucho.

1. _________________________________ (ser)
2. _________________________________ (tener)
3. _________________________________ (comprar)
4. _________________________________ (el)
5. _________________________________ (saber)
6. _________________________________ (gustar)
7. _________________________________ (ir)
8. _________________________________ (mi)
9. _________________________________ (celebrado)
10. ________________________________ (lo)

Nosotros ____1____ de compras. Mi amigo y yo ____2____ comprar ropa ____3____ para ____4____ apertura de clases. Mi amigo quiere un pantalón ____5____ y una camisa con mangas cortas. Yo ____6____ que ____7____ una falda y un par de tenis para ____8____ clase de educación física. Después de ____9____ la ropa, nosotros tenemos que ir a ____10____ supermercado para comprar algunos comestibles.

1. _________________________________ (ir)
2. _________________________________ (querer)
3. _________________________________ (nuevo)
4. _________________________________ (el)
5. _________________________________ (largo)
6. _________________________________ (tener)
7. _________________________________ (comprar)
8. _________________________________ (el)
9. _________________________________ (comprar)
10. ________________________________ (el)

Paragraph Completion (without root words)

Directions: First read the passage and then write, on the line after each number, an appropriate word to complete the passage correctly, logically, and grammatically. Be sure to spell and accent the word correctly. Only ONE Spanish word should be inserted. You will have to use nouns, articles, adjectives, verbs, etc.

A mí ______1______ gusta ir de compras.
______2______ mejor día para ir es el sábado. Tú puedes ir ______3______ centro comercial o puedes ir a ______4______ boutiques. Las boutiques ______5______ tiendas pequeñas especializadas.

1. _______________________________
2. _______________________________
3. _______________________________
4. _______________________________
5. _______________________________

CAPÍTULO 9 ¡Vamos de compras!

Informal Writing

Directions: For the following question, you will write a message. Your response should be at least 35 words in length.

You are writing a note to your brother who is going shopping and you need a few things to cook dinner tonight. You may want to tell him

- what you need
- what store(s) to go to
- what you will be making
- what quantities of each item you need

Formal Writing

Directions: The following question is based on the Sources (**Fuentes**) 1–3. The first two sources are readings. Fill in the graphic organizer when you have finished reading them. You will hear audio material for the third source. Take notes as you listen. Then you will plan your response to the question. Your response should be at least 40 words in length.

¿Qué tipo de ropa lleva la gente en tu región o país? ¿Cómo es similar o diferente a los estilos de ropa en los artículos? ¿Hay gente en tu país que lleva ropa tradicional o indígena?

Formal Writing

Fuente 1 La ropa indígena

La ropa indígena que lleva la población india o indígena de Latinoamérica es muy interesante y muy bonita.

En Guatemala, por ejemplo, la ropa cambia o varía de un pueblo a otro. El traje que lleva una señora de Santiago de Atitlán no es el mismo traje que lleva una señora de Chichicastenango.

La india de Guatemala no lleva sombrero. Pero la india de Perú, sí. Ella lleva sombrero.

La india del famoso pueblo de Otavalo en Ecuador lleva dos faldas de lana oscura con una blusa muy brillante. El señor otavaleño lleva un pantalón blanco, una camisa blanca y un poncho azul.

Formal Writing

Fuente 2 La moda[1]

¿Cómo es la moda en España y en Latinoamérica? ¿Qué estilo está en onda[2]? Pues, es difícil saber. ¿Por qué? Porque la moda cambia rápidamente como aquí en Estados Unidos. Lo que hoy está de moda, mañana está pasado de moda.

Pero podemos generalizar un poco y decir que ahora el estilo favorito de los jóvenes es informal y dinámico. Para los muchachos un blue jean con una camisa amplia[3]. Y para ocasiones más formales—el estilo clásico—el versátil saco azul marino con una camisa azul y pantalones color crema.

Y para las jóvenes hay más variedad y flexibilidad aunque los estilos cambian de un día a otro. En un grupo de tres o cuatro chicas, una puede llevar un traje pantalón con un cinturón sofisticado; otra lleva una falda con una blusa con cuello, abotonada como un saco; y otra lleva blue jean con un blusón.

[1]moda *fashion*
[2]en onda *in*
[3]amplia *loose-fitting*

La moda

En España y Latinoamérica	En tu país

CAPÍTULO 9 ¡Vamos de compras!

Formal Writing

Fuente 3 The following article is titled **Un estilo elegante.**

Voices in the narrative:

Narrator

Write your notes here.

____

____

____

____

____

____

____

____

____

____

____

____

____

____

____

____

____

Informal Speaking 🎧

Directions: You will participate in a simulated conversation. First, read the outline of the conversation. You will have 20 seconds to respond to each question. Once the conversation begins, a tone will indicate when you should begin and end speaking. You should participate in the conversation as fully and appropriately as possible.

You are shopping for a birthday gift for your friend. You are in a store and are approached by a salesperson.

La conversación The shaded lines reflect what you will be hearing on the recording.

La dependienta:	Te saluda y te pregunta lo que necesitas.
Tú:	Le saludas y le contestas.
La dependienta:	Te pregunta sobre la ocasión.
Tú:	Le contestas.
La dependienta:	Te pregunta sobre lo que vas a comprar.
Tú:	Le contestas.
La dependienta:	Te pregunta sobre la talla.
Tú:	Le contestas.
La dependienta:	Te pregunta sobre lo que vas a comprar.
Tú:	Le contestas.
La dependienta:	Te pregunta sobre lo que vas a comprar.
Tú:	Le contestas.

Formal Oral Presentation

Directions: The following question is based on the accompanying printed article and audio selection. First, you will read the article. Then, you will hear the audio selection. You should take notes while you listen. You will then respond to the statement or question below ORALLY.

How is shopping different in your country from the ones mentioned in the sources? Are there similarities? You can begin your presentation with: En mí país la gente va de compras...

Formal Oral Presentation

Fuente 1 De compras en Buenos Aires

En Buenos Aires hay muchas tiendas. Hay centros comerciales, mercados al aire libre, boutiques. Las boutiques son tiendas especializadas. En los mercados al aire libre venden antigüedades y ropa. En las boutiques podemos comprar pinturas, joyas, ponchos y ropa de cuero y lana.

Los mercados o las ferias abren los domingos. La feria más famosa es la Feria de Antigüedades en el barrio de San Pedro Telmo. La Feria de San Telmo comenzó en 1970 cuando un grupo de amigos se reunió por primera vez para vender sus cosas viejas el domingo. Así comenzó la tradición en la Plaza Borrego. Hoy hay 270 tenderetes o puestos donde los vendedores venden sus antigüedades.

Fuente 2 🎧 This article is titled **De compras.**

Voices in the narrative:

Narrator

Write your notes here.

____

____

____

____

____

____

____

____

____

____

____

____

En avión

CAPÍTULO 10 En avión

Short Dialogue 🎧

Directions: You will now listen to an audio selection. You may take notes in the space provided. At the end of the selection, you will be asked some questions about what you have just heard. Select the best answer to each question from among the four choices printed in your booklet.

This dialogue takes place between two friends who are traveling.

Voices in the dialogue:

Announcer, Antonio, Luisa

Write your notes here.

____

____

____

____

____

1
a. en casa
b. en el avión
c. en el aeropuerto
d. en la pista

2
a. Están anunciando la salida de su vuelo.
b. No tiene los boletos.
c. Luisa llegó tarde.
d. No sabe de qué puerta va a salir su vuelo.

3
a. Antonio
b. Fernando
c. Luisa
d. nadie

4
a. Antonio y Fernando
b. Luisa y Antonio
c. Fernando y Luisa
d. Nadie pasó por el control de seguridad.

5
a. Él siempre llega a tiempo.
b. A él no le gusta viajar.
c. Él siempre llega tarde.
d. Él viaja mucho.

CAPÍTULO ⑩ En avión

Short Narrative 🎧

Directions: You will now listen to an audio selection. You may take notes in the space provided. At the end of the selection, you will be asked some questions about what you have just heard. Select the best answer to each question from among the four choices printed in your booklet.

The following is an announcement made aboard a plane.

Voices in the narrative:

Pilot

Write your notes here.

____

____

____

____

____

____

1
a. el piloto
b. el asistente de vuelo
c. el agente de la línea aérea
d. un pasajero

2
a. Caracas
b. Trujillo
c. Carolina del Norte
d. Buenos Aires

3
a. mañana por la noche
b. mañana por la mañana
c. hoy por la noche
d. en dos horas y veinte minutos

4
a. Chile y Carolina del Norte
b. España y Buenos Aires
c. Venezuela y Uruguay
d. Brasil y Uruguay

5
a. veinte
b. dieciocho
c. siete
d. once

CAPÍTULO 10 En avión

Reading Comprehension

Directions: Read the following passage carefully for comprehension. The passage is followed by a number of incomplete statements or questions. Select the completion or answer that is best according to the passage.

This reading is about budgeting and travel.

Si vamos a hacer un viaje, es necesario saber cuánto va a costar. Es una buena idea preparar un presupuesto[1]. El presupuesto nos permite saber cuánto dinero tenemos y cuánto podemos gastar. El presupuesto tiene que incluir los siguientes gastos[2]:

- precio del vuelo
- transporte local
- hotel
- comidas y refrescos
- entradas a museos o teatros

Cuando viajamos, podemos pagar nuestras cuentas o facturas con una tarjeta de crédito, cheques de viajero o dinero en efectivo.

En un país extranjero no vamos a pagar con dólares. Vamos a usar la moneda nacional—pesos o soles, por ejemplo. Tenemos que cambiar dinero. En México es necesario cambiar dólares en pesos. Antes de cambiar dinero, es importante saber el tipo de cambio[3].

Si decidimos pagar el viaje a plazos[4], es necesario saber la tasa de interés que tenemos que pagar.

[1]presupuesto   *budget*
[2]gastos   *expenses*
[3]tipo de cambio   *exchange rate*
[4]a plazos   *in installments*

1 ¿Qué nos indica cuánto dinero tenemos?

a. el tipo de cambio

b. la tasa de interés

c. el presupuesto

d. una tarjeta de crédito

2 ¿Cuál es un ejemplo de un gasto?

a. cambiar dinero

b. pagar el vuelo

c. pagar con un cheque viajero

d. preparar un presupuesto

3 Cuándo viajas a un país extranjero, tienes que usar...

a. el dólar.

b. la tasa de interés.

c. la moneda nacional.

d. entradas.

4 Solo es necesario saber la tasa de interés...

a. si pagas en dinero en efectivo.

b. si vas a cambiar dinero.

c. si pagas con cheques de viajero.

d. si pagas a plazos.

CAPÍTULO 10   En avión

5 La siguiente frase puede estar incluida en el artículo. ¿Dónde la debes incluir?

Todos debemos ser consumidores inteligentes porque la tasa de interés puede ser muy alta.

a. al principio

b. en el segundo párrafo

c. al final del último párrafo

d. al final del tercer párrafo

Paragraph Completion (with root words)

Directions: Read the following passage. Then write, on the line after each number, the form of the word in parentheses needed to complete the passage correctly, logically, and grammatically. Be sure to spell and accent the word correctly. You may have to use more than one word in some cases, but you must use a form of the word given in parentheses. Be sure to write the word on the line even if no change is needed.

¿____1____ tú hacer un viaje en avión? Yo también deseo ____2____ un viaje, pero antes de ____3____ tengo que pensar bien en el viaje. Nosotros ____4____ las maletas. Yo ____5____ la ropa que necesito en la maleta. Después yo ____6____ para el aeropuerto. Traigo todo mi equipaje. Mi ____7____ Juana va a viajar conmigo. Yo paso por ____8____ casa para buscarla. Ella está ____9____ su maleta cuando llego. ____10____ explico que tenemos que llegar al aeropuerto en una hora.

1. _______________________________ (Querer)
2. _______________________________ (hacer)
3. _______________________________ (salir)
4. _______________________________ (hacer)
5. _______________________________ (poner)
6. _______________________________ (salir)
7. _______________________________ (amigo)
8. _______________________________ (su)
9. _______________________________ (hacer)
10. _______________________________ (Le)

Nosotros ____1____ al aeropuerto. Ahora estamos en el mostrador de ____2____ línea aérea. Estamos ____3____ con el agente. Luego, (nosotros) ____4____ al distribuidor automático de donde ____5____ saliendo las tarjetas de embarque. Entonces, tenemos que volver al mostrador porque tenemos que ____6____ el equipaje. Antes de abordar al avión vamos a la tienda para comprar ____7____ regalos para ____8____ familiares. Mi abuelita ____9____ en la Florida. Yo estoy ____10____ en ella.

1. _______________________________ (llegar)
2. _______________________________ (el)
3. _______________________________ (hablar)
4. _______________________________ (ir)
5. _______________________________ (estar)
6. _______________________________ (facturar)
7. _______________________________ (un)
8. _______________________________ (nuestro)
9. _______________________________ (vivir)
10. _______________________________ (pensar)

CAPÍTULO 10 En avión ⋯⋯⋯⋯⋯⋯⋯⋯⋯⋯⋯⋯⋯⋯⋯⋯⋯⋯⋯○

Paragraph Completion (without root words)

Directions: First read the passage and then write, on the line after each number, an appropriate word to complete the passage correctly, logically, and grammatically. Be sure to spell and accent the word correctly. Only ONE Spanish word should be inserted. You will have to use nouns, articles, adjectives, verbs, etc.

Mi amiga Juana ___1___ haciendo su maleta. Ella ___2___ mucha ropa de verano en la maleta porque ella va a la Florida. ___3___ muy buen tiempo en la Florida. Hace calor y hay mucho sol. El taxista pone el equipaje en la maletera ___4___ carro. Ella llega al aeropuerto en taxi. Ella está muy contenta porque a ella ___5___ gusta viajar.

1. _______________________

2. _______________________

3. _______________________

4. _______________________

5. _______________________

CAPÍTULO 10 En avión ··o

Informal Writing

Directions: For the following question, you will write a message. Your response should be at least 30 words in length.

You are writing a note to your friend telling her about a trip you have to take. You may want to tell her

- where you are going
- when you are leaving
- why you are taking the trip
- what you need to pack

Formal Writing

Directions: The following question is based on the Sources (**Fuentes**) 1–3. The first two sources are readings. Fill in the graphic organizer when you have finished reading them. You will hear audio material for the third source. Take notes as you listen. Then you will plan your response to the question. Your response should be at least 45 words in length.

Compara los tres vuelos. ¿Cuál de los tres vuelos prefieres tomar? ¿Por qué?

Formal Writing

Fuente 1 De Nueva York a San Diego

Rebecca García vive en la Ciudad de Nueva York. Ella tiene familia en todas partes de Estados Unidos. Sus primos favoritos viven en la otra costa; viven en San Diego, California.

El año pasado los primos de Rebecca la visitaron en Nueva York, pero este año ella quiere viajar a California. Quiere conocer la casa de sus primos y, por supuesto, quiere conocer el océano Pacífico. Ella va a tomar un vuelo desde el famoso aeropuerto de John F. Kennedy. Pero, no es un vuelo directo. Ella tiene que hacer escala en Phoenix. Tiene que desembarcar y abordar otro avión que va a San Diego.

Afortunadamente sus primos van a estar esperando a Rebecca en el aeropuerto. Ella va a llegar muy cansada después de un viaje de casi diez horas en total.

Formal Writing

Fuente 2 Un vuelo a Europa

Los vuelos entre Estados Unidos y Europa son muy largos, ¿no? El Atlántico es un océano grande. Para cruzar el océano Atlántico toma mucho tiempo.

Teresa Torres está abordando un jet en el aeropuerto internacional de John F. Kennedy en Nueva York. Ella va a ir a Madrid. Es un vuelo sin escala y, después de unas siete horas, el avión va a aterrizar en el aeropuerto de Barajas en Madrid.

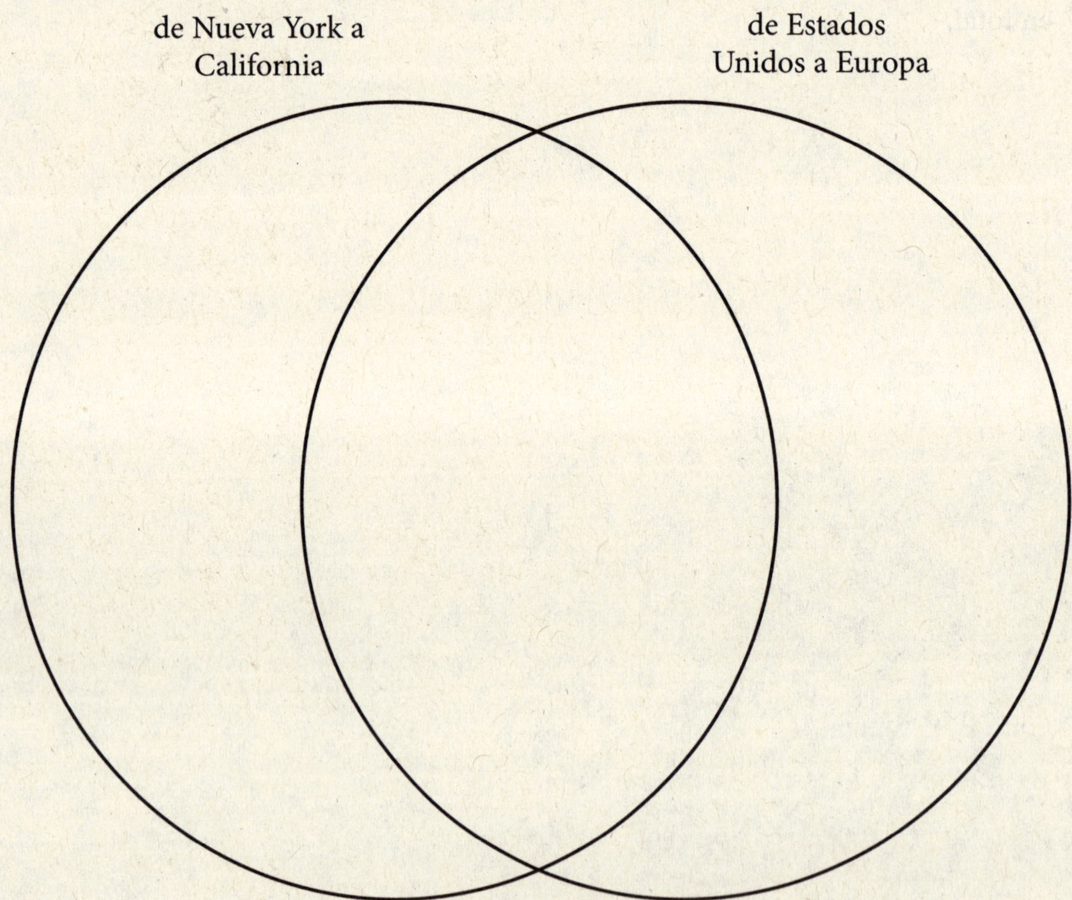

Formal Writing

Fuente 3 🎧 The following article is about flying from Venezuela to Argentina.

Voices in the narrative:

Narrator

Write your notes here.

____

____

____

____

____

____

____

____

____

____

____

____

____

____

____

____

____

CAPÍTULO ⑩ En avión ··o

Informal Speaking 🎧

Directions: You will participate in a simulated conversation. First, read the outline of the conversation. You will have 20 seconds to respond to each question. Once the conversation begins, a tone will indicate when you should begin and end speaking. You should participate in the conversation as fully and appropriately as possible.

You will be taking a trip in a few days and you are speaking with someone from the airline to make the arrangements.

La conversación The shaded lines reflect what you will be hearing on the recording.

El agente:	Te saluda.
Tú:	Le saludas.
El agente:	Te hace una pregunta sobre el viaje.
Tú:	Le contestas.
El agente:	Te hace una pregunta sobre la hora de salida.
Tú:	Le contestas.
El agente:	Te hace una pregunta sobre el viaje.
Tú:	Le contestas.
El agente:	Te hace una pregunta sobre el viaje.
Tú:	Le contestas.
El agente:	Te hace una pregunta sobre la duración del viaje.
Tú:	Le contestas.
El agente:	Te desea un buen viaje.
Tú:	Le das las gracias.

Formal Oral Presentation

Directions: The following question is based on the accompanying printed article and audio selection. First, you will read the article. Then, you will hear the audio selection. You should take notes while you listen. You will then respond to the statement below ORALLY.

Los artículos tratan del avión en la América del Sur. ¿Por qué es el avión importante en esta parte del mundo? ¿Es el avión importante donde vives tú?

CAPÍTULO 10 En avión

Formal Oral Presentation

Fuente 1 Un viaje interesante

Nosotros estamos haciendo un viaje en avión por Sudamérica. Estamos sobrevolando el desierto del sur de Perú. Y, ¿qué vemos desde la ventanilla del avión? Vemos unas figuras muy interesantes. Son las líneas de Nazca. Pues, en el desierto árido del sur de Perú hay una serie de dibujos o figuras misteriosas. Hay figuras geométricas—rectángulos, triángulos y líneas paralelas. Hay también representaciones perfectas de varios animales. A pesar de muchas investigaciones el origen de las líneas o figuras que tienen más de mil quinientos años queda un misterio.

Ahora entiendo por qué el avión es importante. Las líneas de Nazca son tan grandes que la única manera de ver las figuras es por avión.

Fuente 2 🎧 This article is titled **El avión en la América del Sur.**

Voices in the narrative:

Narrator

Write your notes here.

____

____

____

____

____

____

____

____

____

____

____

____

¡Una rutina diferente!

CAPÍTULO **11** ¡Una rutina diferente!

Short Dialogue 🎧

Directions: You will now listen to an audio selection. You may take notes in the space provided. At the end of the selection, you will be asked some questions about what you have just heard. Select the best answer to each question from among the four choices printed in your booklet.

This dialogue takes place between two classmates.

Voices in the dialogue:

Timoteo, Maripaz

Write your notes here.

____

____

____

____

____

____

____

1
a. Timoteo
b. la hermana de Maripaz
c. Maripaz
d. la mamá de Maripaz

2
a. Hoy tiene un examen de inglés.
b. Salió al cine.
c. Timoteo la llamó por teléfono.
d. Hoy tiene un examen de álgebra.

3
a. a las seis
b. a las seis y media
c. a las siete
d. Esta información no está en la conversación.

4
a. la clase de álgebra
b. la clase de inglés
c. la clase de arte
d. Esta información no está en la conversación.

CAPÍTULO 11 ¡Una rutina diferente!

Short Narrative 🎧

Directions: You will now listen to an audio selection. You may take notes in the space provided. At the end of the selection, you will be asked some questions about what you have just heard. Select the best answer to each question from among the four choices printed in your booklet.

This narrative is about ecology and why it is of great interest to everyone around the world.

Voices in the narrative:

Narrator

Write your notes here.

____

____

____

____

____

____

1
 a. Hay grandes campañas de reciclaje.
 b. Las aguas del mundo están contaminadas.
 c. En todas partes hay serios problemas ecológicos.
 d. El automóvil contamina el aire.

2
 a. los gases de los automóviles
 b. las emisiones de las fábricas
 c. los desechos en los ríos
 d. both a and b

3
 a. la plaga
 b. el petróleo
 c. emisiones tóxicas
 d. el equilibrio

4
 a. el papel
 b. el vidrio
 c. el metal
 d. all of the above

CAPÍTULO 11 ¡Una rutina diferente!

Reading Comprehension

Directions: Read the following passage carefully for comprehension. The passage is followed by a number of incomplete statements or questions. Select the completion or answer that is best according to the passage.

This reading is about **el Camino de Santiago.**

Durante la Edad Media[1] hay tres peregrinaciones[2] famosas—la peregrinación a Jerusalén en Israel, la peregrinación a Roma y la peregrinación a Santiago de Compostela.

Santiago de Compostela está en Galicia, una región pintoresca en el noroeste de España. Galicia se parece más a[3] Irlanda que al resto de España. Llueve mucho en Galicia y todo es muy verde.

El Camino de Santiago es el camino que tomaron los peregrinos de la Edad Media. El camino empieza en los Pirineos, en el pueblo de Roncesvalles y termina en Santiago. Atraviesa o cruza todo el norte de España. ¿Por qué quieren ir a Santiago los peregrinos? Porque creen que allí está enterrado[4] el apóstol Santiago.

Los peregrinos viajan a pie de un pueblo a otro. Cada día cubren un trecho[5] fijo. Al final de cada trecho hay un hostal donde los peregrinos pueden pasar la noche. En el siglo XI hay hostales que pueden alojar[6] a unos mil peregrinos.

Una vez más el Camino de Santiago es muy popular. Hoy día muchos turistas toman la misma ruta. Pero no van a pie. Van en carro. Y muchos jóvenes van en bicicleta.

[1]Edad Media *Middle Ages*
[2]peregrinaciones *pilgrimages*
[3]se parece más a *looks more like*
[4]enterrado *buried*
[5]trecho *stretch*
[6]alojar *lodge, accommodate*

1 ¿Dónde está Santiago de Compostela?
a. en Israel
b. en el sudoeste de España
c. en Roncesvalles
d. en Galicia

2 ¿Por qué se parece Galicia a Irlanda?
a. Es muy seco.
b. Llueve mucho.
c. Es muy verde.
d. both b and c

3 ¿Quién(es) está(n) enterrado(s) en Santiago de Compostela?
a. los peregrinos de la Edad Media
b. el apóstol Santiago
c. un apóstol de la Edad Media
d. No hay nadie enterrado en Santiago de Compostela.

4 Hoy día, ¿por qué no van los turistas a pie a Santiago de Compostela?
a. porque van en carro o en bicicleta
b. porque no hay hostales
c. porque toman la misma ruta
d. porque el Camino de Santiago no es muy popular

5 Basado en la información del artículo, ¿a quiénes les interesa tomar el Camino de Santiago?

a. a turistas que quieren quedarse en un hotel lujoso

b. a turistas que quieren ir a Roma

c. a turistas que tienen interés en la historia de la Edad Media

d. a turistas que tienen interés en el arte de la Edad Media

CAPÍTULO 11 ¡Una rutina diferente!

Paragraph Completion (with root words)

Directions: Read the following passage. Then write, on the line after each number, the form of the word in parentheses needed to complete the passage correctly, logically, and grammatically. Be sure to spell and accent the word correctly. You may have to use more than one word in some cases, but you must use a form of the word given in parentheses. Be sure to write the word on the line even if no change is needed.

Unos jóvenes ___1___ están ___2___ de mochileros por la región andina de ___3___ país. ___4___ preparándose para una jornada muy ___5___. Están ___6___ una rutina importante. Tienen que ___7___ los dientes. Ponen sus sacos de dormir en ___8___ mochilas. Después, van a tomar el desayuno. ___9___ a ser un día muy largo, pero los amigos ___10___. Lo están pasando bien.

1. _______________________________ (peruano)

2. _______________________________ (viajar)

3. _______________________________ (su)

4. _______________________________ (Estar)

5. _______________________________ (largo)

6. _______________________________ (practicar)

7. _______________________________ (cepillarse)

8. _______________________________ (el)

9. _______________________________ (Ir)

10. _______________________________ (divertirse)

Mis amigos y yo ___1___ de camping la próxima semana. Vamos a ___2___ una carpa para dormir. También (nosotros) ___3___ un saco de dormir. Yo tengo algunas cosas que ___4___ que llevar en mi mochila. Voy a la tienda de acampar donde compro ___5___ cosas. Necesito cosas para ___6___ higiene personal como ___7___ cepillo de dientes y algunos rollos de papel ___8___. Y como ___9___ frío en las montañas, necesito ___10___ ropa apropiada para el tiempo.

1. _______________________________ (ir)

2. _______________________________ (armar)

3. _______________________________ (llevar)

4. _______________________________ (tener)

5. _______________________________ (alguno)

6. _______________________________ (el)

7. _______________________________ (un)

8. _______________________________ (higiénico)

9. _______________________________ (hacer)

10. _______________________________ (comprar)

Paragraph Completion (without root words)

Directions: First read the passage and then write, on the line after each number, an appropriate word to complete the passage correctly, logically, and grammatically. Be sure to spell and accent the word correctly. Only ONE Spanish word should be inserted. You will have to use nouns, articles, adjectives, verbs, etc.

«Ring, Ring». _____1_____ sonando el reloj. Ana _____2_____ levanta. Inmediatamente ella _____3_____ al cuarto de baño y toma _____4_____ ducha, se lava _____5_____ pelo. Luego, _____6_____ cepilla los dientes. Luego, va _____7_____ comedor donde toma el desayuno.

1. ______________________

2. ______________________

3. ______________________

4. ______________________

5. ______________________

6. ______________________

7. ______________________

CAPÍTULO 11 ¡Una rutina diferente!

Informal Writing

Directions: For the following question, you will write a message. Your response should be at least 35 words in length.

Write a message to your teacher telling him or her why you were late to school. You may want to

- tell what happened
- tell why it happened

Formal Writing

Directions: The following question is based on the Sources (**Fuentes**) 1–3. The first two sources are readings. Fill in the graphic organizer when you have finished reading them. You will hear audio material for the third source. Take notes as you listen. Then you will plan your response to the question. Your response should be at least 40 words in length.

Compara y contrasta los viajes de camping. ¿Cuál de los tres viajes te parece el más divertido?

Formal Writing

Fuente 1 El primer día de vacaciones

La familia Estrella vive en un apartamento en Madrid. El padre y la madre trabajan mucho. Todos los días la familia Estrella piensa en las vacaciones que van a tomar. Esperan el día con mucha emoción. Van a pasar sus vacaciones en un camping en Córdoba, España. Desean estar al aire libre y poder respirar aire puro y fresco.

Por fin, llegó el día de salir. Pero, en el primer día de vacaciones las cosas no pasan como planearon. Primero, descubren que solo tienen una carpa. Entonces toda la familia tiene que dormir en la misma carpa. Y otra cosa más. Está lloviendo y hace mucho viento. La hija menor no tiene ropa apropiada para el tiempo. El hijo mayor sale en bicicleta para ver si puede comprar ropa en una tienda que está cerca. Desgraciadamente, él tiene un accidente y su bicicleta no funciona. Ahora tiene que caminar 10 kilómetros para volver al campamento. Para la cena, la madre prepara unas hamburguesas, pero se da cuenta[1] de que no tiene pan. ¡Qué día más horrible!

Pero, mañana es otro día y están pensando hacer una caminata para disfrutar de la hermosa naturaleza.

[1]se da cuenta *she realizes*

Formal Writing

Fuente 2 En un camping de España

¡Hola! Me llamo Eduardo Bastida Iglesias. Soy de Pamplona, en el norte de España. Para pasar las vacaciones mi familia y yo vamos de camping en el sur donde hace más calor. Por todo lo largo de la costa Mediterráneo hay campings o campamentos. Pero el camping es muy popular y es necesario hacer una reservación, sobre todo en agosto.

Cuando llegamos al camping cerca de Alicante en la costa oriental, levantamos una tienda de campaña. El camping está en una colina. Desde la colina hay una vista magnífica del mar, el cual no está muy lejos. Por la mañana me levanto temprano, me desayuno con una taza de chocolate y unos churros que compramos en el «supermercado» del camping. Me pongo una camiseta, un pantalón corto y los tenis y salgo a dar una caminata por los pinares o bosques de pinos.

Por la tarde, cuando hace mucho calor me baño en el Mediterráneo. De noche me preparo una buena tortilla de gambas. Luego voy a la plaza con mis amigos donde nos sentamos en la terraza de un café y miramos a la gente que pasa.

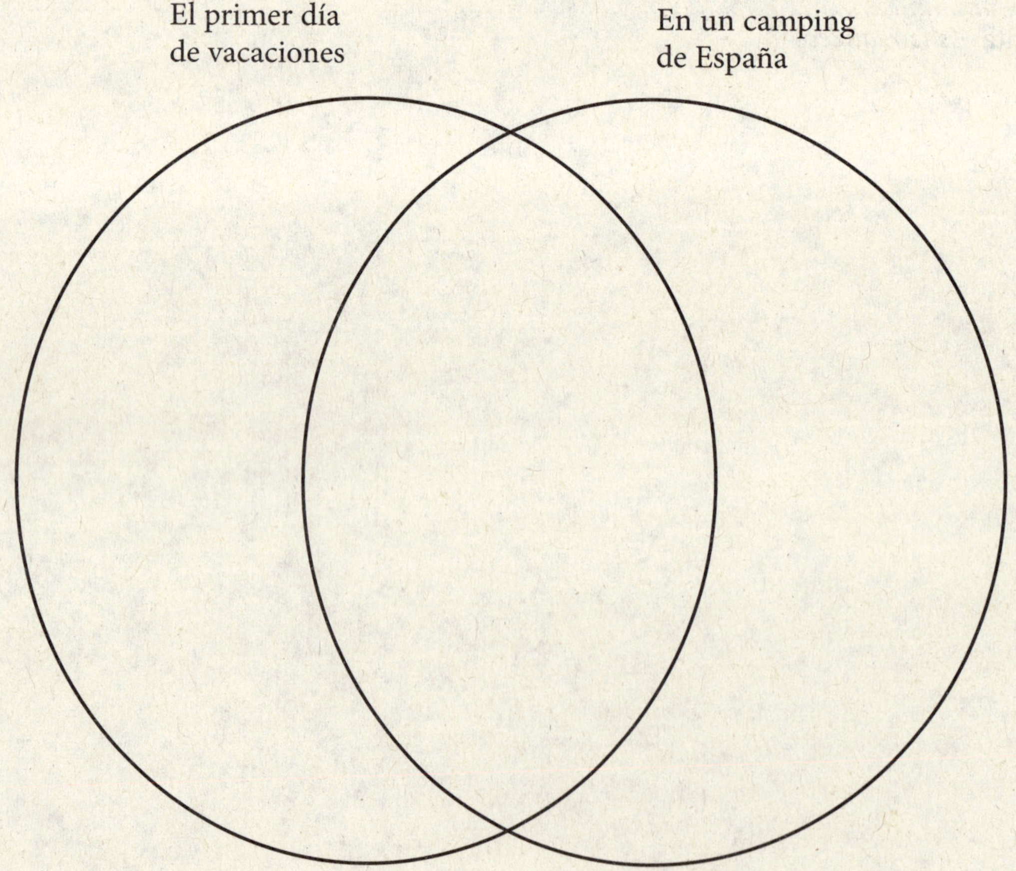

CAPÍTULO 11 ¡Una rutina diferente!

Formal Writing

Fuente 3 This article is titled **Del norte de España.**

Write your notes here.

____

____

____

____

____

____

____

____

____

____

____

____

____

____

____

____

____

____

CAPÍTULO 11 ¡Una rutina diferente!

CAPÍTULO 11 ¡Una rutina diferente!

Informal Speaking 🎧

Directions: You will participate in a simulated conversation. First, read the outline of the conversation. You will have 20 seconds to respond to each question. Once the conversation begins, a tone will indicate when you should begin and end speaking. You should participate in the conversation as fully and appropriately as possible.

You get a phone call from a telemarketer who is surveying people about their daily routine.

La conversación The shaded lines reflect what you will be hearing on the recording.

El agente: Te saluda y te hace una pregunta.

Tú: Le contestas.

El agente: Te hace una pregunta sobre tu rutina diaria.

Tú: Le contestas.

El agente: Te hace una pregunta sobre tu rutina diaria.

Tú: Le contestas.

El agente: Te hace una pregunta sobre el champú que usas.

Tú: Le contestas.

El agente: Te hace una pregunta sobre la crema dental que usas.

Tú: Le contestas.

El agente: Te hace una pregunta sobre tu rutina diaria.

Tú: Le contestas.

El agente: Te da las gracias y se despide.

Tú: Le dices adiós.

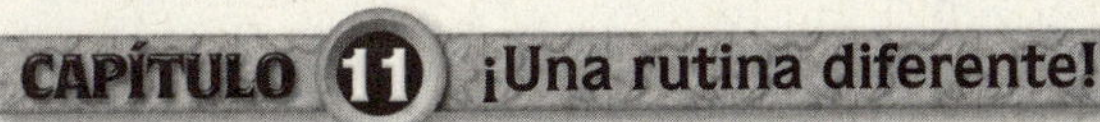

Formal Oral Presentation

Directions: The following question is based on the accompanying printed article and audio selection. First, you will read the article. Then, you will hear the audio selection. You should take notes while you listen. You will then respond to the statement or question below ORALLY.

Basado en la información de los artículos, ¿cuáles son algunas actividades en que participan los campers? ¿A ti te gusta el camping? Explica.

CAPÍTULO 11 ¡Una rutina diferente! ······················○

Formal Oral Presentation

Fuente 1 Me gusta el camping.

A mí me gusta mucho el camping. Siempre voy de camping con mis amigos. Montamos una carpa y dormimos en un saco de dormir. No dormimos al aire libre. Para comer, preparamos hamburguesas y salchichas en una barbacoa. Hay muchos insectos, pero a mí no me molestan.

Nosotros pasamos el día dando caminatas y nadando en el lago. Nos acostamos temprano porque tenemos que levantarnos temprano. Yo soy muy madrugador. Pero hay algo que no me gusta: tener que lavarme con agua fría.

Fuente 2 🎧 The following article is titled **El camping.**

Voices in the narrative:

Narrator

Write your notes here.

____

____

____

____

____

____

____

____

____

____

____

____